I wish I had read this book early in my pastoral ministry. The shock of finding how challenging pastoral ministry could be is honestly faced . . . as is the wonderful grace God provides. . . . Here is a real portrait—both warts and glory—of what it means to be a pastor in the body of Christ.
　　　　　　　　　　　　　　Lester Ruth, Asbury Theological Seminary

Pastors and those who support them need opportunities to see the ministry candidly from the inside. Here is that inside look. This material will be invaluable to all who are involved in ministry in a variety of situations and to those who support and encourage them.
　　　　　　　　　　　　　Howard Vanderwell, Calvin Institute of Christian Worship

Pastoral ministry is done in a cruciform and a person could get hurt doing it! These wonderful essays on the pastoral life, written by brothers and sisters who bear on their hearts the marks of Jesus, will go a long way to help all of us who are called to preach, pray, counsel, and lead in the name of Jesus!
　　　　　　　Timothy Brown, Henry Bast Professor of Preaching, Western Theological Seminary

As I read these testimonies, my first response is sheer gratitude for the tenacious, faithful service of so many pastors. I hope this book not only encourages current pastors but also inspires many of my students to follow their lead.
　　　　　　　　　　　　　John Witvliet, Calvin College and Calvin Theological Seminary

This collection of essays is a treasure. Each is carefully crafted and poignantly written. The authors are more than two dimensional, and their passion for ministry is palpable. Firmly rooted in the Reformed tradition, this volume is a resource that deserves a wide reading across Christ's church.
　　　　　　　　　　　　　Todd E. Johnson, North Park Theological Seminary

Persevering in Ministry

Pastors Tell Their Stories

edited by Joel Kok

Christian Reformed Church in North America
Grand Rapids, Michigan

Unless otherwise indicated, Scripture quotations in this publication are from the HOLY BIBLE, NEW INTERNATIONAL VERSION. Copyright © 1973, 1978, 1984 International Bible Society. Used by permission of Zondervan Bible Publishers.

Persevering in Ministry: Pastors Tell Their Stories © 2004, Christian Reformed Church in North America, 2850 Kalamazoo Ave., SE, Grand Rapids, MI 49560. All rights reserved. No part of this book may be reproduced in any manner whatsoever without written permission from the publisher. Printed in the United States of America on recycled paper.

We welcome your comments. Call us at 1-877-279-9994 X805 or e-mail us at pastoralexcellence@crcna.org.

Cover design by Frank Gutbrod

ISBN 0-9753387-0-6

Contents

Editor's Preface 7
A Note to Readers 9
Contributors 11

In Retrospect

Chapter 1   **The Ministry: What Made Me Do It?**
Louis Tamminga 15

Minister of Word and Sacrament

Chapter 2   **From Grad Student to Disciple**
Joel Kok 27

Chapter 3   **All My Sins Are Washed Away**
Kathy Smith 35

Chapter 4   **Re-Presenting Christ**
Herman Keizer Jr. 43

Persevering Through Hard Times

Chapter 5   **When the Pastor Is Broken**
Len Vander Zee 53

Chapter 6   **In Dependent Independence**
Joel Boot 59

Chapter 7   **Restoring a Lapsed Member and Pastor**
Pedro Aviles 67

Running the Race with Joy

Chapter 8 **Our "Kamikaze" Sailing Adventure**
Richard Sytsma 79

Chapter 9 **The Pastor as Pilgrim**
Cecil Van Niejenhuis. 89

Chapter 10 **On Being a Servant Leader: A Conversation**
Richard E. Williams. 97

Editor's Preface

This collection of narratives is part of a larger project known as Sustaining Pastoral Excellence (SPE). Sustaining Pastoral Excellence is a program funded by Lilly Endowment Inc., that seeks to support pastors so they can help build vital congregations. The SPE implementation team of the Christian Reformed Church seeks to promote healthy pastors and congregations by providing resources for mentoring, peer learning, and continuing education. In connection with these efforts, the implementation team wanted to produce a volume of essays in which pastors would narrate experiences that helped them persevere in ministry. The team hoped these narratives would encourage perseverance on the part of both pastors and congregations; they therefore specified that submissions to this volume should focus on *sustaining* pastoral excellence

The decision to focus on *sustaining* pastoral excellence is a wise one because it relates to the important biblical theme of *hypomone* or perseverance. *Hypomone,* also translated as "steadfastness" or "endurance" or "patience," is a modest but essential virtue for both Christian living and pastoral ministry. According to the apostle Paul, perseverance reflects both the purpose of the Scriptures and the character of God. Paul writes, "For everything that was written in the past was written to teach us, so that through endurance [*hypomone*] and the encouragement of the Scriptures we might have hope." Then Paul offers a prayer to "the God who gives endurance [*hypomone*] and encouragement" (Rom. 15:4-5).

My prayer is that these narratives will encourage pastors to persevere in their calling with a joy that infects their congregations with hope. Jesus' parable of the sower leads me to believe that God will answer this prayer. According to Luke, Jesus describes good-soil people as "those with a noble and good heart, who hear the word, retain it, and by persevering [*hypomone*] produce a crop"(Luke 8:15). Toward the end of this book, Pastor Rick Williams quotes the Rev. Martin Luther King Jr. as saying "everybody can be great because everybody can serve." At the beginning of this book, we can paraphrase the Rev. Martin Luther King Jr. by saying "every pastor and congregation can bear fruit because every pastor and congregation can persevere."

A Note to Readers

At the end of each chapter in this book you will find a section called "For Further Reflection." The purpose of these sections is to encourage you to read and discuss this book in some kind of communal setting. Possibilities for such settings include: pastors and their councils, beginning pastors and their mentors, small groups or book clubs within congregations, seminarians in practical theology courses, groups of pastors who have gathered for mutual edification, and any group of believers who love the church and its leaders. The narratives and the theological reflections embedded in them can stimulate church members to reflect on what God is teaching them as their own stories unfold. Reading this book in community will help accomplish its purpose of promoting healthy pastors and congregations.

Contributors

Pedro Aviles is a second-generation Puerto Rican born in the Latino community of Chicago. He and his wife, Diana, have three children. Pedro has pastored Grace and Peace Fellowship Christian Reformed Church, an inner city Latino church of Chicago, for more than twenty years. In addition, Pedro is the Chicagoland director of the Christian Reformed Church Leadership Development Network and is one of the instructors for the Latino Leadership Initiative.

Joel Boot is currently the Pastor of Preaching and Worship at Ridgewood Christian Reformed Church in Jenison, Michigan. He has been a pastor for thirty years, having served previously in congregations in Le Mars, Iowa, and Dearborn, Michigan. His passion is preaching, and his privilege is worship. He and his wife, Karen, have three married daughters and two grandchildren.

Herman Keizer Jr. retired in 2002 after thirty-four years as a U.S. Army chaplain. He served units in Vietnam and Hawaii and was later a senior staff officer in the Department of the Army and the Department of Defense. Herm was also Command Chaplain in European Command and military advisor to the Ambassador for International Religious Freedom, Department of State. He is currently the Director of Chaplaincy Ministries for the Christian Reformed Church.

Joel Kok was raised in a Christian Reformed family but outside the Christian Reformed subculture. He and his wife, Tricia, have three children. Joel has served Christian Reformed churches in Michigan and Iowa. He currently pastors Trinity Christian Reformed Church in Broomall, Pennsylvania. Joel has also worked as an adjunct professor at three different schools.

Kathy Smith is the Director of Continuing Education for the Calvin Institute of Christian Worship and Calvin Theological Seminary, which involves teaching, preaching, and planning conferences throughout North America. She has served two Christian Reformed churches in Grand Rapids, Michigan, as Pastor of Congregational Life and Ministry Coordinator. Kathy and her husband, Doug, have three daughters.

Richard E. Sytsma spent eight years of his youth as the son of missionaries to Japan. He served with InterVarsity Christian Fellowship and then became a Christian Reformed missionary in Japan from 1968-2000. He is currently Dean of Students and International Student Advisor at Calvin Theological Seminary. Rich and his wife, Sandra, have three children and two grandchildren.

Louis M. Tamminga was born in the Netherlands. He was pastor of congregations in British Columbia, Alberta, Iowa, and Ontario before becoming Director of Communications for Christian Reformed World Missions (CRWM). Lou then served as Director of Pastor-Church Relations for the Christian Reformed Church in North America (CRCNA). In retirement, he serves as pastor to missionaries of both CRWM and the Christian Reformed World Relief Committee (CRWRC). Lou and his wife, Jean, have five children, nine grandchildren, and one great-grandchild.

Leonard J. Vander Zee was ordained in 1970. He has been pastor at the South Bend Christian Reformed Church for nearly fourteen years. Previously, he served congregations in Iowa, New York, and Michigan. He is married to Jeanne Logan and has four grown children and six grandchildren. His forthcoming book, *Christ, Baptism, and the Lord's Supper*, will be published this year by InterVarsity Press. Len's current passions include golf and hiking.

Cecil Van Niejenhuis enjoys crossword puzzles and golf. He has served four Canadian congregations, two in Ontario and two in Alberta, in his twenty-three years of parish ministry. He is currently pastor of First Christian Reformed Church in Edmonton. Cecil and his wife, Karen, have three grown children.

Richard E. Williams has served since 1981 as the pastor of Pullman Christian Reformed Church, a multiethnic congregation in the Chicago metropolitan area. He and his wife, Amalia, are originally from Panama. They are the parents of three grown daughters and have four grandchildren.

In Retrospect

CHAPTER 1

The Ministry: What Made Me Do It?

Louis Tamminga

When people aspire to the ministry they desire "a noble task" (1 Tim. 3:1). However, ministers are subject to the same temptations that beset Jesus' disciples and the Pharisees. They can easily argue among themselves about who is the greatest. They can do all their deeds to be seen by others. In this piece, Louis Tamminga examines his own motives in a way that testifies not only to our need for grace but also to the triumph of grace even among those with mixed motives.

Once upon a time I had what I thought was a good ministry experience. I visited a woman of our church in the hospital, talked with her, listened attentively to an account of her illness, spoke words of encouragement, read the Bible with her, and prayed with her. Then, before leaving, I made the rounds in her ward. I stopped at each of the ten or so beds, inquired about each patient's well-being, and expressed my hope for a speedy recovery. As I left, the woman of our church assured me that what I had just done had surely blessed those women and had enhanced the reputation of the church. I smiled my " 'twas nothing" smile and made my way home.

I would have forgotten this little event, if not for something else that happened a few hours later. As I entered the parsonage that afternoon, my wife, Jean, met me at the door with worrisome news. "Karen is sick," she said. "She has a high fever. I have phoned the doctor, and he will come to the house soon." Karen was our little daughter, the only girl in a family of boys, and an amazingly intelligent and affectionate child. The doctor's diagnosis was not long in coming: appendicitis requiring immediate surgery.

So, that afternoon I visited the hospital a second time, now together with my wife. Much of it was the same. The same hallways, the same gleaming floors, the same odors, the same nurses, the same sounds—yet how different it had become. Earlier that afternoon, I had made my little glory round, innocuous and disingenuous as it was. Now I was part of a frightening reality—our little girl extremely sick, eyes closed, face flushed with fever.

After an hour's waiting, a nurse came over hurriedly. "Her appendix," she said, "is ruptured, and the operation will take longer." We anxiously inquired about the prospects of success. She assured us that the doctors were very capable and would do what they could. Jean and I waited, prayed, and clung to each other. "Lord, this little girl must not die, she means the world to us. Lord, please." More waiting, more anxiety, more prayers; then the surgeon came over, his face sweaty, his eyes tired, his mask dangling below his chin. "She will be O.K." he said, "she is a sick little girl but she'll make it."

Oh, the enormity of the relief!

"Thank you, thank you, thank you, Lord!"

Did I learn from this experience? Had I become a different hospital visitor? Had I become a humbler minister? Could I now relate honestly to the many other visitors who worried because their loved ones suffered and were in pain? I cannot really remember, but every now and then it hit me as I hurried through the hospital corridors: I am now in the temple of suffering, fear, and pain. As I think back to ministry experiences such as these, I realize again how complex the motives were that prompted me to serve. None of them were wholly bad, but even the best were tainted with self-centered concerns.

Ministry and Motives

I should have been forewarned. I had read and even preached from John 12, where Mary poured the pure nard on Jesus' feet as a loving ministry deed offered to the Savior. Simple directness! Pure motives! Then there is Matthew 20, where, not long afterward, the mother of James and John (and she loved and served Jesus . . .) approached Jesus with a request: "Grant that one of these two sons of mine may sit at your right and the other at your left in your kingdom." Status charms the godliest. Motives are rarely totally pure. To serve for no other reason than simple Christian love, I found, is an ideal at once precious and elusive.

Jean and I were in Haiti some years ago for a variety of get-togethers with our missionaries. One of the missionaries took us for a walk around a neighborhood in Port-Au-Prince. On one street corner, we saw an old woman surrounded by children who appeared to listen to her intently. The missionary motioned us to sit down on a low section of wall nearby. We realized that the woman was teaching. The missionary said, "She is teaching the neighborhood children stories from the Bible; she does it every morning." I found myself asking typical minister questions: "Is she sponsored by a church? Is she being paid by someone to do this work?" The missionary said, "No. She simply loves to teach the Bible, and she loves the children."

Jean and I have often thought of that woman in Haiti. From God's point of view she probably ranked high as a dignitary in the church. Would I preach and teach if I did not have a church that honored me, looked after me, challenged me, and surrounded me with resources and benefits? True, I toiled over sermons; I delivered them as well as I could, and I think I loved the worshiping congregation. So, yes, from one point of view my motives for the pulpit ministry seemed to be O.K., but did I recognize all the other dubious little motives that clung to the central love-motive the way possum babies cling to their mother's back? How much ministry did I do because it was expected of me or because it rewarded my work with some acclaim (be it ever so fleeting) or because I had a need to be part of something significant or because I had a need to be in the center of things or because my arguments were a bit original and even interesting or because preaching affirmed me in my religious convictions and professional choices?

All these bits of interwoven motives became part of how I habitually worked. I think I hardly recognized the less-than-godly motives for what they were. The distress of that, I came to see, was that I became insensitive to the effect of dubious motives. I didn't even feel the pain that resulted from some ministry acts too much designed for getting a lot of work done and firming up my professional standing in the church world.

Looking back now, I realize how hard it is to recognize and identify the mixed motives from which I served—some good; some not so good; and some, well, bad. That afternoon in the hospital, visiting out of sense of duty, I gladdened the hearts of some suffering people. Much kingdom work is done from a sense of duty, and what's wrong with a sense of duty? Didn't the grandmother in Haiti tell Bible stories from a sense of duty? I realized however, that it's not that simple. Must not a sense of duty be sanctified? Christ, I have increasingly come to see, manifests himself especially through those who serve from holy motives. The grandmother in Haiti served because her love for Christ was genuine. As she told Bible stories to little children, she sensed the presence of Christ. Did I, perhaps, in my ministry fail to cultivate the presence of Jesus in what I undertook and who I was?

Examining our motives can wake us up to our need for grace and the presence of Jesus. Grace will flourish when we cultivate the presence of Christ. Grace will enable us to do ministry in his power and to dedicate it to him.

Two Points to Ponder

The absence of grace creates, I believe, two fundamental shortcomings in the practice of ministry: (1) the organizational and institutional aspect of the church assumes inordinate importance and makes incessant demands for maintenance and results, and, therefore, (2) ministers rely on their own professional competence to the point where they find it hard to avoid manipulation rooted in idolatry. These two shortcomings have a common root: too little trust in Jesus.

More on the first point: When the institutional church, with its privileges and rewards, gets an alluring hold on those who maintain it, the church itself can become an obstacle to the free course of grace.

In 1950, I attended a meeting in the city of Amsterdam at which the Rev. J. Overduin related his experiences in the Dachau concentration camp during the Second World War. (He later wrote a book about these experiences, and he was often quoted from pulpits.) "On Sundays," Overduin said "we were not allowed to be together with more than three prisoners in one group. That last winter we would hunker in the snow leaning on one another, and we would recite texts we knew from memory. We would reassure each other of Christ's promises, and we would say prayers. And that's when we realized that we were a very basic expression of the New Testament church: believers in the presence of their Savior. Rarely had we experienced the presence of Christ so closely." Three people in the snow, reduced to nothing but themselves and Jesus, and, therefore, totally church. This is what Overduin added: "In spite of that blessed assurance, I kept missing the privileges of the ministerial office . . . . It was a painful struggle to lay that last holdover of a good life into his hands. And it was disconcerting," he said "how soon after coming home I became used to those privileges again."

I can relate to that. I have also found that the very size and prominence of congregational structures tend to absorb too much of church leaders' spiritual vitality. Loving, personal, one-to-one care then becomes increasingly difficult.

I once met a Vietnamese minister who told me how he had ministered for nearly three years in a refugee camp. He had been the only pastor of a growing number of Christian believers. "We had no books, no study sources, and no paper, so I kept no records and did no administration," he said. He then explained that, in spite of those terrible limitations, a surprising amount of pastoral work took place. In fact, the limitations added to his pastoral effectiveness. He devoted his time chiefly to spelling out the gospel to anyone who would listen. He related to everybody as a father or a brother, and those who believed told others about the good news. The very limitations made him deeply dependent on Jesus, whose presence he experienced constantly. He then proceeded to tell me that he had been allowed immigration into the United States and had become the pastor of a Vietnamese congregation. "What joy it was," he said "to have a building and study sources and meeting spaces and discussion groups and transportation." Then he added, "I lost something too: So much of my time now goes into keeping the organization going, I have become the keeper of an institution, and it is now more difficult to do ministry in the company of Jesus."

I heard a minister quote Eugene H. Peterson: "The biblical fact is that there are no successful churches. There are, instead communities of sinners gathered before God week after week. . . . The Holy Spirit gathers them and does his work in them. In these communities of sinners, one of the sinners is called pastor and is given a designated responsibility: to keep the community attentive to God."

Peterson, of course, simply echoes the genius of the sixteenth-century Reformers insofar as they rediscovered the church to be people, a communion of forgiven saints relating directly to God in Christ. Salvation by grace alone! The priesthood of all believers! I knew these slogans but did not always practice them. I had enough spiritual sensitivity to be deeply concerned about the spiritual well-being of my parishioners and, indeed, of my own. The reality was that the needs of the church as an institutional entity were startlingly real. The same held for the several Christian organizations and denominational committees in which I was involved. Not meeting those needs had very unpleasant results. So, much of my attention went into caring for institutions. The duties that demand most of a pastor's time and attention can easily become a way of life. Moreover, as many ministers will testify, tending the organization well is rewarded with congregational approval.

Closely related to all this, I found, was the penchant I had to see results in my ministry. Where my inner certainty was not fully affirmed by the closeness of Christ—in other words, where I functioned only partially from grace—I mistook blossoming church life for spiritual fruits. In fact, I mistook congregational well-being for my own spiritual health. These forms of idolatry have insatiable appetites. I needed to have something to show for all my efforts. So, I worked hard to create ideal situations of peace and harmony. Because so much depended on my efforts, I took vacations with reluctance. I wanted all the members to be happy. I wanted every committee to function efficiently. I insisted that the elders made their rounds, that teachers taught well, and that the deacons looked after the needy with dispatch. It's amazing how tolerant, even appreciative, consistories were of this type of ministry. It seemed everybody loved a well-oiled machine.

A process such as this never stands still. It demands more and more from the pastor, and I was not above some manipulation to keep the machine going. Not the mean kind, of course. I practiced the gentle, wise kind of manipulation—a well-timed compliment, some advice carefully repeated, a little prodding, lining up the right people for just the right situations, a warm word of appreciation. At the time, I was not fully aware of it, but somehow, already during my early ministry, I began to address symptoms rather than causes. Removing symptoms brought (seemingly) quicker results than dealing with causes. That, I found out, suited church members just fine—at least initially. I became adept at solving problems. I had a way of mediating conflicts. I sometimes said things people wanted to hear in order to gain their cooperation. I loved peace. I developed a distaste for confrontation.

I must clarify that sorting out motives is not simple. There is a good side to being concerned about the smooth functioning of the church, and there is a good side to being concerned about results in the ministry. I have heard ministers fulminate against the business model being foisted on them by business-oriented elders, and I have sympathy for their feelings. The church is not a for-profit business, but that does not mean that ministers should not be held accountable for the use of their time or that they should not seek to acquire new skills and better methods. The point is whether we recognize the sources from which we draw. Is our source the grace of Christ or our own ambitions? Or perhaps we should ask: Do my ambitions serve Christ, or do I try to make Christ serve my ambitions?

What I have been describing here is less a confession of sin than a recognition of tendencies of which I was only vaguely aware. I think I may say that my ministry was prompted by love for Christ, that I did find strength in personal prayer and in studying the Scriptures, and that throughout my ministry years there were re-awakenings. Somehow the Spirit opened my heart to sweet intimacy with Christ. That, I think, was reflected in my preaching, and that, I now see, fed the congregations I served. Although I failed sometimes to live up to Paul's words, "we walk by faith, not sight," Christ's Spirit kept me in a state of grace in spite of myself

Means of Grace

Looking back, I can also see that the Spirit saved me from myself in other ways. He brought godly believers to my path that enhanced the reality of grace in my life and ministry. Simply by who they were and how they lived, they challenged me to have an honest look at my inner life.

The first such person was my wife Jean. The Lord has endowed her with purity of heart. Her inner life seems to dovetail with Christ's grace effortlessly. She asked the hard questions in a harmless way. Her motives were always transparent; for her, there just was not another way to be and to live. In matters of stewardship and diligence I could keep up with her in my own way, but what sometimes amazed me was that it seemed so natural to her to leave the outcome in the hands of the Lord. Neither of us was free from worry, but while she waited on the Lord, I ran ahead of the Lord. The beauty of her presence in my life was that she ascribed her own motives to me.

There were, of course, others, too many to mention here, who modeled for me dependence on the Lord. Here I must tell you of a group of people with whom I met during a season of CPE (Clinical Pastoral Education) training at Pine Rest Christian Hospital. The group in which I was placed was chaired by the Rev. James Kok, then a chaplain at Pine Rest. Our group was composed of pastors, chaplains, and other caregivers, both women and men. Their credentials were held by a variety of evangelical churches. We would consider all sorts of pastoral situations, and Jim would draw out how we proposed to minister in each. He was particularly concerned for us to understand our motives for serving. No amount of inner pain or turmoil the group members expressed seemed to cause him much discomfort as long as they were expressed honestly. He seemed to thrive particularly on disagreements that might surface among group members as a way to come to a clearer self-understanding.

I was probably the slowest to catch on. As soon as the participants explained their problems and struggles, I would rise to the occasion. I would rephrase each one's situation in more favorable terms. When someone would reveal a weakness or a failure, I would sketch the other more favorable side of her person and conduct. When someone expressed disagreement with a fellow group member, I would quickly come with an explanation that made both parties look acceptable. My standard phrase became: "what you really mean is . . . " and, voilà, the weakness and problems looked much more respectable.

One day, the group applied a mini intervention on me. I remember the scene well. I was placed in the middle of that small circle. The questions began innocuously enough, but the pressure soon mounted: How was I doing? Did I struggle with difficulties? Was I ever unhappy? Did I always feel good about myself? Did my feelings never bother me? Was I ever angry? Why did I always come to everybody's rescue . . . ?

I began to feel uncomfortable.

My self-confidence began to waver.

The questions kept coming; more direct now . . .

Do you think that you must save us from ourselves and from each other? Do you always try to solve everybody's problems? Why do you wrap your kind explanations around the honest failures we express here? What are you hiding under your edifying words? What do you do with your own pain? You seem to have a lot of fear inside you; why are hiding it so scrupulously? Where do you take your anger? Are you afraid to face yourself honestly? Must you always look good?"

The rest is not easy to relate. It is enough to say that I broke down, had a glimpse of my inner make-up, and found healing in the embrace of honest believers who themselves had all been where I had roamed so long.

I remember another thing about these CPE sessions. I came to realize that what they confronted me with was no secret to me. I had known those things all along. I was close enough to the Word of God to be faced, now and then, with the troubling question: Was my ministry work truly approved by God? The more painful instances of that struggle were when they hit me deep within: What if I missed the boat completely? What if this was not at all how the Lord intended to build the church?

I know other ministers have had such moments of crisis.

I once met a woman at a church-doing somewhere. She told me that I must have known her father from previous contacts, and I did indeed remember him well. He was a godly pastor; what she then told me, I did not expect. Her father, she said, had gone through terribly painful spiritual struggles toward the end of his life. This is how I remember her words. "Dad was such a good man, such a wonderful father, such a humble, caring minister. But on his sickbed, he was attacked by racking doubt and fear. At times he trembled with anguish that he had failed miserably. My mother would sit close to him and wipe the beads of sweat from his pale forehead, and she would assure him that Christ was his Savior and that he would let no one pluck him out of his hand. In the end, grace triumphed, and he died in peace."

I pondered that woman's words. If that modest, humble pastor could be so guilt smitten, where would I be?

Before graduating from Calvin Seminary, Dr. John Kromminga gave the senior class a brief farewell address. In it, he said something to the effect that when we would shake hands with the people after the service and someone would say, "That was a great sermon, pastor," we should accept it gracefully and gratefully. Everyone needs a compliment now and then. "But," he said "remember then that without Christ's suffering and death there would be no sermons for which people could praise you."

Someone asked me whether, if I could live my life over, would I choose the ministry again. I had to think for a moment. I said, yes, I thought I would. I have found the ministry truly fascinating and not without rewards. I have also found it difficult and demanding. Would I have done better if I had known what I know now? Probably not. The same weaknesses would have clung to my best efforts. However, I also know that Christ would have accompanied me all the way.

The ministry: What made me do it? The grace of Christ that I found so hard to live by fully was, I now know, behind it all.

For Further Reflection
Compare Tamminga's reflections with Paul's statements: "I worked harder than all of them—yet not I, but the grace of God that was with me" (1 Cor. 15:10), and "I no longer live, but Christ lives in me" (Gal. 2:20). What are ways pastors can "set aside the grace of God" (Gal. 2:21)? How can examining our motives for ministry make us able to claim with Paul, "his grace to me was not without effect" (1 Cor. 15:10)?

Minister of Word and Sacrament

CHAPTER 2

From Grad Student to Disciple
Joel Kok

*According to the ordination/installation form for ministers in the Christian Reformed Church, "The preaching of the Word is one of the minister's chief tasks." The form then goes on to describe various other urgent tasks that can compete with sermon preparation. However, the form also offers a clue for integrating these many tasks when it states, "In **all** [emphasis added] his work, the minister proclaims, explains, and applies Holy Scripture in order to gather in and build up the members of the church of Jesus Christ." Apparently, proclaiming Scripture includes but is not limited to preaching and the academic study that goes into good preaching. In this piece, Joel Kok reflects on discipleship as a way to find integration and joy as a minister of the word.*

One of the pivotal events in my pastoral life is one that did not happen. In February of 2001, I was interviewed for a position as professor of Church History at Calvin Theological Seminary. After a lot of soul-searching, I solemnly decided that I could, in good conscience, leave pastoral ministry and accept this academic position. However, God had other plans, and the seminary faculty offered the position to someone else.

Since that time, I have reflected on the teaching dimension of the pastoral calling. These reflections, combined with some revelatory experiences and a few key books, have led me to make discipleship central to my life and work. Discipleship has offered me clues for how my academic training fits into Christ's mission. Discipleship has expanded my understanding of Christian learning and has helped me to see how my love for learning can express itself in love for the church. Discipleship has taught me to testify, if I may paraphrase Psalm 1 this way: "Blessed is the pastor whose delight is in the ministry of the word."

Theology in a Junkyard

One of the delights that the ministry of the Word offers is the way in which it involves pastors and congregations in God's creation-wide work of redemption. This sense of being involved in "a great project" (Neh. 6:3) came home to me in an odd way one morning during my seminary days when I visited a junkyard.

I had lost the gas cap to my car and thought the junkyard was a logical place to buy a replacement. The gate was open, so I walked fifty yards or so into the yard, calling out for someone who worked there to assist me. Unfortunately, the only employee I met did not understand my benign intentions. As I stepped behind one of the abandoned cars, I came face to face with the proverbial junkyard dog.

My idiotic cries for assistance turned immediately into terrified cries for rescue. Snarling, the watch dog flew at me and pursued me back toward the entry gate. At the gate, the dog actually took my legs out from under me, but my forward momentum led me to slide head first through a large mud puddle and onto a patch of gravel just beyond the reach of his chain. There, I sat up and, in a state of near shock, watched the brute strain to break his collar so he could finish me off. A few moments later, I realized that my glasses had slipped off my face and had sunk into the depths of the mud puddle, but grief for this loss was more than offset by relief for my life having been spared.

The theological message embedded in this incident came out in a somewhat embarrassing thought that flashed through my mind as I ran for my life. Even as I was shouting in fear during my six-second sprint, one part of my mind kept thinking: "This can't be happening. I simply cannot die in this junkyard. After all, I'm a promising young seminarian."

The exaggerated sense self-importance this train of thought reveals needs no commentary. However, I hope the grace of the moment shines through as well. As a seminarian, I was not particularly important, but I was undergoing training for the most important mission there is: God's mission to make the kingdoms of the world into "the kingdom of our Lord and of his Christ" (Rev. 11:15). God's plan in Christ encompasses "all things" (Eph. 1:10), and to participate in this plan as "pastors and teachers" (Eph. 4:11) is a humbling honor for ministers of the Word. It is an exciting delight to spend time preaching and teaching Christ as he rules over the universe and sends the church to "make disciples of all nations" (Matt. 28:19).

Glorious Things of Thee Are Spoken

My interest in preaching and teaching goes back to my freshman year at Calvin College when my eyes were opened to the rich world of Christian scholarship. In an introductory philosophy class during that year, I did some reading in Augustine's *City of God,* and this book prompted me both to profess my faith publicly and to declare myself a "pre-sem" student.
I remember hardly any of the content of this reading assignment, but I do remember the thrill of encountering Augustine's towering Christian mind. During my public high school days, I had picked up a vague notion that people were religious during the Dark Ages, but when the Enlightenment came we put away such childish things, at least as far as public life and learning were concerned. When I read Augustine in a Christian college setting I had two primary responses. First, that this was the most comprehensive depiction of reality I had ever encountered; and second, that I wanted to tell everyone about this world and life view. I became convinced that people who do not love God with all their minds do not know what they are missing. So I decided to get this message out by becoming a minister.

My love for Christian learning did not waver during my college years, and it continued during my seminary years. As graduation from seminary approached, I decided to apply to graduate programs in religion. I was accepted into the History of Christianity program at Duke University in 1986 and finally completed my dissertation in 1993. By that time, I was the pastor of Unity (now called Trinity) Christian Reformed Church in Ames, Iowa. Both in Ames and in Broomall, Pennsylvania, my second charge, I resolved not to treat church work as a steppingstone to an academic position. I realize now, however, that deep down I did expect to wind up teaching at Calvin Seminary. When that did not happen, I began to rethink how my academic training fits into my work as a pastor. This rethinking led me to look back with gratitude on lessons I had learned when I was still enrolled in graduate school but was also working for a church.

And He Had Compassion on Them

While researching and writing my dissertation, I worked for two years as a part-time youth minister for Second Christian Reformed Church in Grand Haven, Michigan. During my second year at this position, the beloved senior pastor, Gene Los, accepted a call to another church, and I became the primary pastoral figure in the congregation. In retrospect, I see this as a significant time in my journey from graduate student to disciple. Both from the example of the senior pastor and from my experiences with church members, I learned lessons regarding the primacy of love.

I should explain that I came to Grand Haven with what I now call a grad student chip on my shoulder. At Duke, I had studied the relationship between Christ and culture with Stanley Hauerwas, who was on my dissertation committee. I had wrestled with Anabaptist critiques of Reformed ecclesiology. I had done a lot of reading, and I judged that Christians in the United States were far too compromised by the materialistic society in which they lived. I believed they had a lot to learn about the mission and identity of the church, and I also figured I was the one to tell them what they needed to know. I don't want to exaggerate my attitude at this time. I believe I was polite and friendly enough, but I did need to discipline my mind to what John Calvin called "a teachable frame," and a couple of incidents can illustrate how people at Second Grand Haven helped me to overcome at least some of my arrogance.

One day, I met an elderly member of the church while we were both shopping in a grocery store. When she saw me, she apologized for having missed church the previous Sunday, and she explained her absence. Late Saturday night, she told me, her husband had lost control of his bowels, and she had worked into the wee hours of the morning cleaning and caring for him and washing sheets. These activities had left her too tired to come and hear me preach.

Another incident took place one evening when an elder accompanied me on a home visit I had arranged. Fairly quickly I got into an argument with the father of the household about his failure to attend church regularly. After several minutes of fruitless exchange, we lapsed into an angry impasse. The elder then took over the lead in the visit, and his sympathy for the family elicited from them a description of the mixed feelings they had about church and the judgmentalism they sometimes experienced there. This elder then offered a moving prayer on behalf of the family, and as he prayed, Christ became palpably near.

My pastoral education continued in January of 1991, when the Gulf War broke out. I led two adult Sunday school classes about different Christian attitudes regarding war and peace. While describing the just-war position, I advocated the pacifist position, which I held at that time, and my opposition to the war came out also in my sermons and prayers. This led to a few heated exchanges with church members, but mostly my fellow believers at Second Grand Haven listened to me with courtesy and a humble desire to hear God's word on this difficult question. After one evening service, in which I had offered a prayer that was probably too politically partisan, an elder named Ron Kuiper gently said to me, "You are militant in your pacifism." He spoke the truth in love and also with a sense of humor and perspective.

In his book, *Freedom for Ministry,* Richard John Neuhaus sums up a lesson he learned from the Rev. Martin Luther King Jr. King used to say: "Whom you would change, you must first love." That sums up the lesson I learned from these and other incidents at Second Grand Haven. My academic studies truly had prepared me to teach the congregation many things. I had a lot to learn, but I also had genuine teaching gifts to offer. However, my arrogance, flowing from a lack of love, was the first obstacle I had to overcome in order for this teaching ministry to bear fruit. As Paul says, "Knowledge puffs up, but love builds up" (1 Cor. 8:1). Paul's instructions in 1 Corinthians 12-14 also apply here, and I'll quote one salient verse: "Follow the way of love and eagerly desire spiritual gifts, especially the gift of prophecy"(1 Cor. 14:1). I continue to struggle with Christian attitudes toward war and peace, but I have learned that true prophets do not despise the people of God. They love the church, and they speak the truth in love.

I think that my experiences at Second Grand Haven are worth passing on because I believe arrogant contempt poses a besetting temptation for many pastors. Because we take church life seriously, we can become seriously frustrated church people. When we succumb to the temptation of angry contempt, we harm our congregations and defeat ourselves. We need to remember: We cannot change people we do not love. Learning to follow Jesus' teachings with respect to anger and love was a major lesson I began to learn in Grand Haven, and this was an important step in my journey as a disciple.

Liable to the Hell of Fire

While most of the people at Second Grand Haven treated me with courtesy, a few were less than perfect in the way they offered criticism. The most significant incident in this regard took the form of an angry phone call I received one evening that left me first stunned and then furious. The caller actually had a legitimate point about an area in which I had been remiss, but his invective was disproportionate to my offense. He later apologized, but in the meantime I nursed both my wounds and my anger.

For a few days, I devoted many of my waking hours to formulating speeches that combined self-defense with counterattacks. I was considering the best time to return the phone call, but, thank God, I first called a friend, Gary Van Dalfsen, who had become a Christian counselor. I described the conflict and its context; I explained that I did not want to keep my rage bottled up in some unhealthy way, and, in effect, I asked permission to berate the fellow who had berated me. Gary listened sympathetically and then asked, "What do you want to happen?"

As I sputtered toward a response to that question, I began to realize that mostly I wanted to hurt the other fellow as badly as he had hurt me. Beneath the arsenal of self-justification I had constructed, the truth was as simple and as sinful as that. The more I consider how this conflict could have escalated and infected the whole church, the more I see the wisdom of Jesus' teachings regarding anger and retaliation. This incident did not end with everyone living happily ever after; the brother and I did not reach full-scale reconciliation. We did, however, manage to avoid fratricide, and for that I'm grateful. I think of the sun rising on Jacob as he limped toward his partial reconciliation with Esau, and I thank God for blessing those who limp imperfectly in the direction of perfect love.

The temptation to lash out in anger continues to beset me. Sadly, I sometimes translate my anger at church members into impatience with family members. Someone criticizes me gracelessly, and I'm more likely to yell at my kids over breakfast. A group fails to appreciate my best efforts, and I can become preoccupied and grouchy. I find it revealing that the Lord confronted Cain after Cain and Abel had brought offerings to the altar. I believe the Lord's question to Cain is a good one for pastors and all church leaders to ask themselves: "Why are you angry" (Gen. 4:6)?

There is such a thing as righteous anger, and righteous anger can energize us for good works. Even righteous anger, though, must be subject to love, and unrighteous anger, which is often rooted in wounded egos, must be crucified. I like the New American Standard Bible's translation of the Lord's warning to Cain: "If you do well, you can hold up your head; but if not, sin is a demon lurking at the door; his urge is toward you, yet you can be his master" (Gen. 4:7, NASB).

The two writers who have most helped me to understand my anger in light of Jesus' teachings are Dietrich Bonhoeffer and Dallas Willard. Dallas Willard's work, *The Divine Conspiracy,* includes a masterful treatment of anger, and the entire book offers a wealth of wisdom that speaks to all people but can also speak specifically to pastors and other church leaders about persevering in their labors even when they experience frustration. Willard's emphasis on Jesus' intelligence is especially significant for pastors who wonder how their academic theological training can serve the practical demands of church work. *The Divine Conspiracy* was pivotal in my journey from grad student to disciple. It makes me grateful for my academic training, which is essential to pastoral work. It also encourages me to supplement academic training with the many forms of learning by which people become disciples of Jesus.

As helpful as Willard is regarding anger, love, and learning, I'll let Bonhoeffer have the last word in this section. I'm thinking here not of *The*

Cost of Discipleship, but, rather, of his book, *Life Together. Life Together* is a classic treatment of ministry, and it includes a priceless warning against the destructive power of what Bonhoeffer calls "wish dream" visions. Wish dream visions are graceless, egotistical ideals for church life that lead pastors to love imaginary congregations more than the actual congregations God calls us to serve. Bracingly, Bonhoeffer states, "God hates visionary dreaming. It makes the dreamer proud and pretentious. . . . So he becomes, first an accuser of his brethren, then an accuser of God, and finally the despairing accuser of himself."

The Love You Had at First

Having reflected on the primacy of love for pastoral work, I should also confess that I'm still learning to find the proper balance between love in the form of pastoral care and love in the form of sermon preparation and study. In a book called *Preaching about the Needs of Real People,* David Read reflects on this balancing act by using the image of the ambidextrous preacher. The idea is that preachers need to minister with both hands; that is, they need to combine enthusiasm for biblical texts with interest in people and their lives. Read, like many others trained during the heyday of neo-Orthodoxy, began his ministry concentrating on exegesis and without much concern for whether parishioners could understand him. He sees a parallel in some of the social-justice preaching of the 1960s in which preachers would use certain texts to attack rather than to instruct some of the more conservative members of their congregations. Writing in the 1980s, however, Read argues that the pendulum has swung too far the other way. Preachers are now too prone to neglect the Word in order to address people's problems in direct but unbiblical ways.

Read is probably right about the pendulum swing, and he is certainly right about the need for pastors to be ambidextrous. To carry the image a little further, pastors can ask themselves: Which arm am I allowing to atrophy—the study arm or the caring arm? In my own case, I know that when I allow the study arm to atrophy, not only do my sermons lose effectiveness, but I also begin to lose enthusiasm for my work. When this happens, I need to hear the message our Lord gave to the angel of the church in Ephesus: "I know your deeds, your hard work and your perseverance. . . . Yet I hold this against you: You have forsaken your first love. . . . Repent and do the things you did at first" (Rev. 2:2-5). For me, the things I did at first include Bible study and the more general forms of reading that made me want to become a minister in the first place.

I believe most pastors and councils would do well to discuss the extent to which the pastor's schedule allows time for meditating on God's Word.

I believe congregations that encourage their pastors to spend significant time in sermon preparation and in general studies will gain better sermons and become healthier bodies of Christ. Encouraging pastors to practice love in the form of study will infect the congregation with joy in God's Word. As Psalm 1 teaches, meditating on God's Word brings delight, and as Psalm 150 promises, such delight in God's Word serves God's plan to "let everything that has breath praise the Lord. Praise the Lord" (Ps. 150:6).

And Gladly Would He Learn

One more aspect of discipleship that sustains me as I search for balance in the pastoral life is the promise that as I struggle with how to follow Jesus even in such things as the nuts and bolts of time management, Jesus will teach me not only through his words in the Bible but also through his gracious presence. When I gather with even one or two other disciples in Jesus' name, he promises "there am I with [you]" (Matt. 18:20). As the church I pastor wrestles with everything from worship to doubt to paying ministry shares as a form of mission to all nations, Jesus keeps his word: "And surely I am with you always, to the very end of the age" (Matt. 28:20). Jesus can teach me through the snarl of a junkyard dog and through the *Confessions* of Saint Augustine. Truly, to lose my life for Jesus is to gain life. My hope for myself and for all pastors is that people can say (supplying their own inclusive language) of us what Chaucer said of the clerk in his *Canterbury Tales:* "And gladly would he learn, and gladly teach." But, I should give the last word to the Master himself. What Jesus says to his disciples in Matthew 13 applies in a special way to pastors: "Therefore, every scribe who has been trained for the kingdom of heaven is like a householder who brings out of his treasure what is new and what is old" (Matt. 13:52 RSV).

For Further Reflection

How does academic training differ from discipleship? How can academic training equip pastors as disciples?

In terms of the ambidextrous preacher image, do you (or your pastor) need to do more exercise with the study arm or the caring arm? In what specific ways does your congregation encourage its pastor to meditate on God's word? Is continuing education for the pastor built into the congregation's life?

CHAPTER 3

All My Sins Are Washed Away
Kathy Smith

Sometimes, pastors and congregations eager to do ministry see the Church Order as an obstacle to the gospel. What can rules and regulations do except obstruct the grace and love that are central to the church's ministry? Yet, rules can be a gift from God because, as Paul wrote: "For God is not a God of disorder but of peace" (1 Cor. 14:33). In this piece, Kathy Smith demonstrates how pastors and elders can express love in the form of an orderliness that edifies the church.

"All my sins are washed away!"

That's what four-year-old Zachary said to me when I asked him if he understood what baptism means. I was on my knees talking to him at eye level, just ten minutes before the worship service in which I was to baptize him. I wanted him to see who I was before this happened because we had not met before. So, I said to him, "Hi, Zachary, my name is Rev. Smith, and I'm going to baptize you this morning. Do you know what that means?"

After he gave the answer that showed how much he already knew about baptism, I asked if he knew what I was going to do to him.

"Put water on my head!" he said with a grin. "Three times!"

Then his grandma, standing behind me, prompted him: "Tell her what she's going to say when she does it, Zachary."

"Oh, I know! In the name of the Father . . . and the . . . Son . . . and the . . . ," he hesitated. Now it was my turn to prompt him.

"In the name of the Holy . . . ," I paused.

"Spirit!" he shouted triumphantly.

After we talked a bit more about what was going to happen in church that morning, I stood up and noticed that Grandpa had caught the whole conversation on videotape! Grandpa and Grandma were just two of the many family members who had come to church that morning for Zachary's baptism—the baptism that almost didn't happen.

Questions and Obligations

It was an awkward situation. Zachary's parents, Steven and Mary, had heard that another couple in the church was having their baby baptized on Sunday because they had family in town for the Memorial Day holiday weekend. They, too, had family around, which wouldn't be the case later in the summer when they had originally planned to have their new baby baptized—Zachary's little sister Ellie. So, they called the church to ask if they could be included in the baptism service too, and the worship committee representative said, "Sure!"

Because our regular pastor had retired months before and no replacement had yet been found, I received a call from the first couple asking me to administer the sacrament of baptism to their baby girl. I readily agreed, not yet knowing about the second family involved or how many more phone calls would be placed before Sunday arrived. As an associate pastor, I don't often have opportunities to administer the sacraments. So, I was looking forward to this occasion almost as much as the parents were!

The worship committee member didn't realize that there are questions to ask when it comes to baptism. Also, there are certain issues of church polity and church membership that need to be clarified in a denomination like ours, which has agreed on certain ways of doing things such as this.

In this case, the first couple who requested baptism had been church members for a long time. The father had even grown up in the congregation. Their two other children had been baptized in our church, and now the third was ready. So, it seemed like "standard procedure."

That was not true of Zachary's parents though. They had been attending the church for quite a while but had not become members. Thus, when the elders were informed of the plans for the upcoming baptisms, they started asking questions. When they contacted me, I raised even more questions! Finding the answers would have been easier if there had been more time available, but it was already Wednesday, and the baptism was scheduled for Sunday. The family was already planning on it and inviting guests to the worship service.

The question for me then became: How can I respond pastorally to this family and to our congregation while honoring the covenant promises that I made as an ordained minister to "do the work of my office faithfully . . . in submission to the government and discipline of the church?" I had obligations to my church family and to my denominational family and also to this new family that I wanted to welcome into the church.

A Joyful Reaffirmation

The "complications" in this baptism situation had to do with membership status and family make-up. Steven and Mary had been married for about a year and during that time had started attending our church. Then baby Ellie was born, joining a family that already included Mary's son, Zachary. The congregation celebrated Ellie's birth with them, having already come to include them in the church family.

Neither the parents nor the elders realized that the upcoming baptism would raise so many questions: What was the membership status of the parents? Had they actually joined the church? Was their membership transferred from another church? Were they both church members? What about little Zachary? Was he now the son of both parents? Did his new dad have legal authority over him?

These seem like technical questions, the kind that church clerks and church polity folks think about. They are, however, also important issues in a church that baptizes the children of believers under the promises of God's covenant. In our denomination, children are not baptized according to their personal faith. They are baptized and received into church membership on the basis of God's covenant, which is extended to them through their parent's membership in the church.

Therefore, due to all the questions that had come up, I was asked to clarify some issues with the elders and the family. In addition, I wanted to respond to this new family in a way that would draw them closer into our church, not push them away. There was a lot at stake here—the possibility of alienating an entire family. It took several phone calls, but eventually we had some results.

The first question was answered when it was determined that the father had made profession of faith in a nearby Christian Reformed Church and just the week before, thinking of the impending baptism, had requested a transfer of his membership. The elders of that congregation met and approved the transfer, which was then faxed over to our church. That meant that the new baby Ellie could be baptized and that Steven could answer the questions put to parents of covenant children in the baptism ceremony. We weren't yet sure if Mary would be able to answer the questions along with him.

Then again: What about Zachary? We knew he was Mary's son, but we didn't know if Steve had adopted him or had any legal rights to him. Furthermore, we still didn't know if Mary was a church member. If Steve had no legal rights and Mary no church membership, I would not be able to baptize Zachary.

Besides all these membership questions, I raised the important pastoral one. Who is meeting with these parents to prepare them for baptism? Do they understand the sacrament and its meaning? Are they willing and ready to make the commitment—actually, the profession of faith—that is required in the form for baptism?

After a series of phone calls with the elders (while I was on vacation attending my own daughter's sporting event in another state), we decided that we needed to meet with Steven and Mary to clarify things and also to help them understand the issues and the importance of the questions we were asking. Although time pressured us because of the plans already laid for the Sunday morning baptism service, another elder and I set up a meeting with them for Saturday at 9:00 a.m.

I was prepared to pull out all the pastoral stops in helping them through this situation, knowing that I might have to recommend they wait with Zachary's baptism—wait until either his stepfather became his legal father or until his mother became a church member. Knowing they would be disappointed if we couldn't allow the baptism, I was also ready to recommend that they wait with the whole business until this could all be straightened out and they could do all this as a family. Then the elders could take time to meet with them and properly disciple them into church membership. Of course, I knew it would not be an easy message; the grandparents, the aunts, the uncles, and the soloist had already been invited and lined up.

We met at the church; the parents seemed a bit nervous. They didn't know the elder, but they did know me from seeing me in church and having a few conversations after previous services. I started out by welcoming them and asking them to tell us a bit about their lives—both their personal stories and their faith journeys. We already knew the status of the father in regard to membership and baptism. I was eager to learn about Mary's story, and then on hearing it, to determine what we should do next.

The story was interesting and encouraging. She had been born in a Christian Reformed family—a pastor's family, in fact! Her father had baptized her as an infant in a Christian Reformed church. She had not made profession of faith in a Christian Reformed church, though. When she grew up, she had moved to another state. While living there she gave birth to Zachary and searched for a new church but didn't find any Christian Reformed churches around. So, she and her new little son started attending a Church of the Nazarene nearby. She wanted her son to grow up in the faith. This congregation welcomed them, and eventually she went through classes to become a member and professed her faith in that church.

Later she had moved back to Michigan to be nearer family and friends and had she met and married Steven. Although Steve wanted to adopt Zachary, and Zachary considers him his father, adoption procedures had not been possible due to lack of agreement from the birth father.

As we talked, it became clear that Mary wanted to be a church member along with Steve, and that her profession of faith was sincere, although it had not happened in a Christian Reformed church, and we had no record of it.

When I explained why we needed to ask all these questions and how this could affect their plans, they began to realize that it wasn't a sure thing that Zachary would be baptized on Sunday. Steve suggested that maybe they should just wait with the whole business. I could see he wasn't happy about it, but he wanted to do things right, and he wanted their children to be baptized together. So, I thought about it, and the elder, realizing I needed to make a decision, indicated that he would support my choice.

I said to them, "Normally, the elders and I would want to spend time with you, preparing you for the baptism and for Mary to make a reaffirmation of her faith. We would probably get together with you over a period of time." Then, if that process led Mary to reaffirm the profession of faith she made in another church, she would be received by the leaders of this church as a member. In order to baptize Zachary with integrity, that step needed to be taken. Keeping in mind the plans this family had made while they were unaware of the questions we would be asking (and should have asked sooner), I made a decision. I asked Mary if she would be willing to meet with the elders on Sunday morning (the next day) to reaffirm her profession of faith. She didn't have to, but the option was there. I knew the elders would be willing to meet with her, and I was pretty sure she and Steve would want to do things properly, although a bit rushed!

That's what we did. Early Sunday morning a group of six elders and I met with Mary and listened to her story—a wonderful story of a faith journey that seemed to wander away from God and family for a time but eventually came back. Knowing that she would be professing her faith again when she answered the questions put to parents in the baptismal form, I decided to ask her to reaffirm her faith before the elders by answering the questions asked in the form for profession of faith.

She did that. They were touched by her story and the reaffirmation of her faith. They welcomed her into the church family as a full member—based on her baptism and profession of faith in a Christian church. We offered a prayer of thanksgiving, and gave warm hugs all around. Then Mary went to get baby Ellie ready for the service, and I went to see Zachary and talk to him about baptism.

That special moment was just a preview to the baptism event itself. I had the wonderful privilege of announcing to the congregation that we would administer the sacrament of baptism to three covenant children that day. I explained that John and Rachel were presenting their third child, Emma Rebekah, for baptism, and that Steven and Mary were presenting their two children, Zachary Joseph and Ellie Catherine. I explained how Steve's membership transfer had been received from a neighboring Christian Reformed church and how the elders had met with Mary to hear a reaffirmation of the profession of faith she had made in the Church of the Nazarene. I explained that all of their families were present, including Mary's father, who had baptized her as an infant in a Christian Reformed church not too far away.

I could tell that the congregation appreciated the information and was rejoicing to hear that Mary and Steven had both been received by the elders as new members of our church. Then we proceeded to the baptism. I asked "profession of faith" questions of both sets of parents:

"First, do you confess Jesus Christ as your Lord and Savior, accept the promises of God, and affirm the truth of the Christian faith which is proclaimed in the Bible and confessed in this church of Christ? Second, do you believe that your children, though sinful by nature, are received by God in Christ as members of his covenant, and therefore ought to be baptized? Third, do you promise, in reliance on the Holy Spirit and with the help of the Christian community, to do all in your power to instruct these children in the Christian faith and to lead them by your example into the life of Christian discipleship?"

I baptized Emma Rebekah as her parents and two big brothers looked on. Next came Ellie Catherine, who was baptized while Zachary and Steven and Mary watched. Finally, Mary held Zachary close to the font, and I said to him, "Zachary, I'm going to baptize you now, just like we talked about." He smiled and I proceeded: "Zachary Joseph, I baptize you in the name of the Father and of the Son and the Holy Spirit, Amen." I rested my hand on his forehead with the blessing. He looked up at me with another one of his big smiles and said, "You dripped all over me!" My lapel microphone caught his comment, and the whole congregation heard and laughed lightly.

One of the elders presented the parents with miniature baptism banners to hang in their children's rooms to wait for occasions to tell the story of their baptism and what it meant. Of course, Zachary had firsthand knowledge of his baptism. I think he will remember that day for a long time. After the service he came running up to me during the coffee hour in the fellowship hall and tugged on my skirt. I smiled at him and lowered myself to his eye level again.

"Thank you for baptizing me!" he said with a big grin. The hug he gave me is something that I will never forget.

Rewards of Being a Team Player

What does this all have to do with sustaining pastoral excellence?

Pastors are sustained in their work, not just when things are going smoothly, but more often when a difficult situation turns out well because of the timely and discerning use of their pastoral gifts. Being effective, doing the right thing, solving a problem without sacrificing the people involved, creating a wonderful congregational moment that could have been awkward at best and painful at worst . . . ; these are things that sustain pastors.

They aren't as tangible as a string of good comments at the door following a sermon. They do, however, give the lasting satisfaction of knowing that you played well on God's team that day. He pitched a curve ball to you, and you not only connected with it; you hit a home run. The satisfaction of being used well by God through the gifts he has given sustains the pastor from within and that's where it really counts. A pastor can get a lot of warm fuzzies from the congregation and still feel empty and inadequate inside. When you know in your heart that you followed the Spirit in a touchy situation, the good feelings will sustain you in your passion for ministry.

That goes for associate pastors too—ministers who do pastoral work in "specialized ministries," not in a typical congregational parish setting. They need to be sustained in ministry in the same way as parish pastors. Perhaps they need it even more because they don't always enjoy the support of a congregation that both affirms them and holds them accountable.

Recently, our congregation interviewed a man who was a candidate to be the next pastor of our church. When asked about his favorite thing to do of all the things a minister does, he talked about the honor and privilege of administering baptism. He became very animated as he spoke of how amazing it is to be able to play that role on behalf of God and the church. I thought: *How cool it would be for more associate pastors to be able to share in that joy and excitement!* Maybe congregations should think about including their associate pastors more often in the administration of the sacraments, including opportunities to serve the Lord's Supper.

Whether they feel it or not, all pastors are sustained in ministry when they follow the patterns agreed upon by the denomination. Even if it takes some scrambling and some extra phone calls and meetings to get answers, it's worth the time to get it right. Congregations will respect a careful process more than a quickly patched-together approach—especially when things as important as sacraments and church membership are involved, not to mention families and feelings. These are also great learning opportunities for the leaders of the church as well as the members.

At the end of the day, it doesn't get much better than to have a four-year-old smile up at you and say, "Thanks for baptizing me!"

For Further Reflection

Consider Paul's concluding statement in 1 Corinthians 14: "But everything should be done in a fitting and orderly way." Try dividing these instructions into two commands:

1. All things should be done.
2. Do all things in a fitting and orderly way.

Do you and your congregation emphasize number 1 or number 2? In other words, do you need more spontaneity or more orderliness? What dangers attach to each when the other is ignored?

Consider also your relationship to the denomination of which you are a part. Do you tend to see other members and churches in your denomination as teammates, competitors, or referees?

CHAPTER 4

Re-Presenting Christ
Herman Keizer Jr.

All believers live in a battle zone, and God commands us all to put on the full armor of God in order to take our stand against the evil one (Eph. 6). In this piece, Herm Keizer calls on his military and combat experience to explore the power of God as manifested in sacrament and symbol.

Evil has its own fascination and attraction. Even when it frightens us, evil can seduce, allure, mesmerize, titillate, and compel. A visit to the Holocaust Museum in Washington, D.C, or to the concentration camps of Dachau in Germany or Auschwitz in Poland provide graphic proof of evil's power to fascinate. Museum visitors look in silence at the horrors on display. At first they avert their eyes, but then the initial shock or shyness fades, and they focus on all the details—fascinated and transfixed.

I visited Auschwitz in 1995. Scenes from *Schindler's List* came vividly into my memory as my mind filled the stark latrines and barracks with the ghostly images of the film. The European chaplains and I were silent, sober, and transfixed by the sights of the place. Even as we read the warnings and heard the plea, "We must not let this happen again," we knew of new detention camps in the Balkans with names such as Djeneral Jankovic, Glogovac, Srbica, and Vucitrn. Even as we watched the repulsive reminders of the holocaust, we were living in the world of ethnic cleansing. Again, we watched in horror, feeling incapable of acting to stop evil in its tracks.

September 11, 2001, swept us up into a maelstrom of horror displayed on television screens and in newspaper pictures. The same events, repeated over and over, assaulted our senses again and again. Even those of us who were close to the rubble and devastation of that terror-filled day were also caught up in the fascination and excitement of seeing evil and its children run amuck on our national stage. People could not leave their viewing perches, lest they miss another happening. The face of evil mesmerized.

Evil can fascinate on the small stage as well. People in an illicit relationship feel the wrongness—the evil—of their acts, yet they persist. The blush of romance, the excitement of cover-up, and the drama of secret rendezvous all have their allure, and the clandestine planning has its own spy-thriller fascination. Even when the affair has lost its glow and become uncomfortable, evil continues to exert its power. Memories of the excitement and the wish to recover it continue to seduce.

Watch a child sitting in the backyard with his back to the house as he looks furtively over his shoulder to see if his parents are watching. He pulls matches from his pocket and lights one. He hides the glow and waves his arms to dissipate the smoke. Another glance back at the house. Another match lit and burned longer. Another and another lit and discarded. No hands wave away the smoke. Finally, another's hand rests lightly on his shoulder. Caught! Caught up in the act and mesmerized by the fire, his initial caution disappeared like the smoke of the match.

The power of evil is its ability to grip us. We do not often see the horrible face of raw evil, but even when we do, it compels us. Evil is powerful, and it takes a decisive power to defeat it. God in Christ has won the decisive victory over evil and all its forces. My experience as a chaplain has given me insights into how we Christians have access to that victory and its power.

The Lord's Supper in Vietnam

My early ministry was in a place where evil showed its rawest face—the battlefields of Vietnam. Riding in my jeep down Thunder Road, Highway 1, in Vietnam in 1969 and stopping at a tank or armored personnel carrier, presented a ministry challenge. Soldiers were standing guard in tanks and armored personnel vehicles every quarter mile or so, each vehicle within eyesight of the next. Each had fewer than a handful of soldiers standing guard to protect the road from being mined. The duty was filled with boredom; laced with hidden fears. Too much time to do nothing but read and sleep, listen to Armed Forces Radio-Vietnam, take your turn at watch, then read and sleep again. Yet, the boredom was spiced by the threat that a rocket grenade could zoom its way out of the tree line, smash into your position, and leave you and/or your friends dead.

How do you minister to such soldiers in a meaningful way? My predecessor had told me that at first he would stop, hand out Bibles and literature, talk a bit, and move on. Later, he stopped doing even that because the soldiers all had Bibles, did not read the literature, and seemed uninterested in talk. So, he would stop only occasionally, make some small talk, and move on.

During my second week in Vietnam, I stopped by a tank and visited with some of the soldiers. Many had not been to chapel in weeks. I asked if they would like to have a short communion service. They said yes, so I got out my chaplains kit and set it up. We held a brief service, just the three of us. When I broke the host and gave it to them, they were respectful and thoughtful. As I said the words, "the body of Christ broken for you" and "the blood of Christ shed for you," the other soldier, who was not attending, turned off the radio. It was a quiet and reverent moment. I told them that, after having seen death in combat, they probably knew more vividly now about the power of death to break a person. Death was powerful, but life in Christ was more powerful. I witnessed to the resurrection. Christ had beaten death.

After the service, they thanked me. One said that this communion service had a richer meaning for him because he had seen some friends killed in an ambush. "Jesus understands all the fear, the temptation and the horror that comes with facing death. Knowing that he knows is a comfort." I stopped at the next two track vehicles and had some small talk. At the next vehicle, a soldier asked me if I would serve communion. He told me he had talked to his friend on the radio and his friend had told him about the service. He had three others who also wished to join in the communion service.

That night I spent a great deal of time reflecting on those two services. The meaning of the sacrament was vivid here in a war zone in a way different from in the safety of churches back home. These young men had seen the broken bodies of their fellow soldiers. They had seen bodies with little wounds where the bullet entered and huge fleshless holes where the bullet exited. They had seen limbs blown away by mines and booby traps. They had seen death in some of its rawest forms. Death was not antiseptic, cleaned up, and neatly dressed. Death was a brutal breaking of the human person.

Because these services were so meaningful, I decided to ask more often if soldiers wanted the sacrament. The positive response surprised and overwhelmed me. The more I worshiped around the sacrament, the more touched I was by the power of the elements to tell the gospel message.

Here I was, a chaplain from a church that did not see the sacrament as a daily or weekly or even monthly worship practice, wanting to offer this sacrament again and again. My church trusted me to admit to the Lord's table only those who professed Christ as their Savior. The concern for the sacraments goes back in the history of Christian Reformed Church to the inception of sending ministers of the Word into the military as chaplains in World War II. The discussions then concerned the ability of our ministers to serve as chaplains and still honor our heritage regarding the role of sacraments in the life of the church. We had a high view of these means of grace, and I did not want to detract from the precious experience of the Word as sacrament. I felt the trust of the church and took that trust very seriously. I struggled with the question of how often to celebrate the sacrament.

I rehearsed in my mind what we believed about the sacraments. I had few resources with me in the field, so I relied on memory, contemplation, and prayer. The Heidelberg Catechism was a great help in my contemplation.

Q. 75 *How does the Lord's Supper remind you and assure you that you share in Christ's one sacrifice on the cross and in all his gifts?*

A. In this way:

Christ has commanded me and all believers to eat this broken bread and to drink this cup. With this command he gave this promise:

First, as surely as I see with my eyes the bread of the Lord broken for me and the cup given for me, so surely his body was offered and broken for me and his blood poured out for me on the cross.

Second, as surely as I receive from the hand of him who serves, and taste with my mouth the bread and the cup of the Lord, given me as sure sign of Christ's body and blood, so surely he nourishes and refreshes my soul for eternal life with his crucified body and poured-out blood.

Q. 76 *What does it mean to eat the crucified body of Christ and to drink his poured-out blood?*

A. It means to accept with a believing heart the entire suffering and death of Christ and by believing to receive forgiveness of sin and eternal life.

But it means more. Through the Holy Spirit, who lives both in Christ and in us, we are united more and more to Christ's blessed body. And so, although he is in heaven and we are on earth, we are flesh of his flesh and bone of his bone. And we forever live on and are governed by one Spirit, as members of our body are by one soul.

What the soldiers received from my hand was the nourishment their souls needed for eternal life. The marriage language in the answer to Q. 76 struck me. The God of the promise unites us with Christ in such an intimate way that we can cry like Adam, "This is now bone of my bone and flesh of my flesh." These visible signs are a pledge that his sufferings and obedience are definitely ours, so much so that they are as if we personally suffered and paid for our sins.

My concerns about "May I?" changed to "How can I not?" It would not be right to deny these powerful assurances to these soldiers who faced the possibility of death in combat. God was assuring them that they were part of a kingdom that was eternal and that they would receive his promises as surely as they received these elements.

I served the Lord's Supper at every service possible from that time on. In combat, Sunday was whichever day the chaplain showed up. In the field and in the base camp, every day was the day the Lord had made, and my soldiers and I rejoiced in the comfort that came from seeing his body broken for the forgiveness of our sins and for a participation in the banquet of the Lamb. We celebrated this powerful reality in worship, praising God for the power to raise us up, through our baptism into his eternal life. We had been baptized into his death. The service with the sacrament brought that death and resurrection to our remembrance.

I also found in the sacrament a new humility. I continued to struggle with the soldiers as we tried to obey the command, "Love your enemies." How can you possibly love someone who just killed your buddy or killed innocent people in a village simply because they received medical assistance from an American military doctor? Words of power did not come to me. I was often speechless in my own rage as I prepared for yet another memorial service. Love for enemy was not always in my heart as I wrote a mother and father or a young wife that a son or husband was dead. Those who were killed by a personnel mine or a boobytrap caused me to feel the most resentment against the enemy. I was humbled by the message of the sacrament that pointed to a Jesus who forgave his taunting killers from the cross. How eloquent a message! The elements were a sign pointing to an enemy-forgiving Savior, but they were also a symbol. The symbol called and empowered us to do the same as Jesus did. Forgive! Forgive! Forgive again and again!

In many other settings, I discovered the power of the sacraments to express in symbols more than ministers can put into words. I decided to claim the power of the symbols that God has given in the sacraments and to let God use them to tell the marvelous story of his saving work in our world. God came to be buried and to rise, to damn sin and to bless life, to give us new life and to sustain that life with the food of the kingdom. The food of the kingdom is the fruit of the Spirit. This fruit builds a community of faith—always striving to be faithful, always lacking perfection, but always relishing the perfection of God's redemption through Jesus of Nazareth, the Christ of God.

I continue to find in the sacraments a power for proclamation and care for the soul. In a service recently, a family, who had their own biological children, presented a minority child they had adopted for baptism. The child's biological mother was present in the service, and her presence was acknowledged. The church's universality and catholicity were present in the service, and no one needed to say that we were seeing an extraordinary act of God's love in the church and in his world.

The sacraments tell this story so well. When they speak, it is time for me to be silent!

The Power of Symbols

My experience in the military alerted me not only to the power of the sacraments but also to the power of symbols in general. As a military chaplain, I learned to "read" symbols in a way that helped me understand this community and its mission.

I have been with commanders as they sat at the map table with a flat map, filled with all the symbols necessary for reading a terrain's many features. They discussed such things as line of vision, the risk of exposure for troops in that position, the possibilities for ideal cover and concealment, and lines of march for troop movement. They could visualize the entire terrain from the map symbols. They knew what the symbols meant and could translate those symbols into concrete plans. I moved with these commanders from the map table to a helicopter and flew over the ground they had described at the map table. It was amazing to see how accurate they were in sizing up the advantages and disadvantages of the terrain. After spending time studying maps, I, too, became proficient at reading the symbols. This ability gave me status with soldiers and commanders. I belonged to their profession and could demonstrate proficiency in the skills of the trade.

A soldier's uniform is filled with symbols. We call them accoutrements. There are many different accoutrements, and all of them have a meaning. You can learn a lot about soldiers just by looking at the uniform. You can tell their current unit, branch, what unit they served with in combat, what their rank or grade is, how many tours they served overseas, what regiment they belong to, what combat operation they were on and where, and what individual awards they have earned. The soldier displays past history and current status. All information is available at a glance—if you know the symbols.

On my uniform, I wore a cross—the symbol that I was a Christian chaplain. The cross is a powerful symbol. The symbol, though, does not convey the true horror of the death that came to those hanging from these instruments of torture. I have read many accounts by experts of the excruciating pain that accompanies death by crucifixion. The accounts are very chilling.

However, the cross is more than a symbol of a death suffered. It conveys much of the Christian story. See the cross and you see a loving, creating Father who is not abandoning his world to its own destruction. You see God becoming like us, putting on our human flesh, living a life of obedience, forsaken by friends, betrayed, killed, and miraculously resurrected. You see the living reality of a church with a mission to be Christ's presence in the world, empowered by the Spirit of the living Christ.

I find that astonishing! As the church, we make Christ present to the world.

As I reflect on my ministry in the military, I have been amazed by the power of the symbol and by the power of bearing that symbol. I was a minister of the Word sent by my church to make Christ present in a place where my church could not go. I did not build a church. I worshipped on battlefields, in beer halls, in mess tents, in beautiful chapels—in any place and at any time. There were no elders or deacons, no membership roles, no building committees and funds—none of the usual things associated with church. Wherever we worshipped was a chapel. This reality is associated with the origin of the word for chaplain and the nature of ministry as a presence.

Chaplains and a Ministry of Presence

The word *chaplain* comes from the Anglo-Norman and Old French word *chapelain* and from the Medieval Latin *cappellanus,* which was originally associated with the guardian of the cloak of Saint Martin of Tours. The story goes like this:

Martin of Tours was riding on his horse when he approached a beggar who was scantily dressed. Martin took out his sword and cut his cloak (*cappel*) in half and gave it to the beggar. That night he had a dream that the beggar was the Christ. The cloak became a relic that was carried into battle. The keeper of the cloak was the *cappellanus*—the one who carried the cloak of Saint Martin of Tours. Since then, chaplains have been the keepers of sacred things.

Chaplains have long talked about their ministry as a ministry of presence or an incarnational ministry. Because the chaplain is a keeper of sacred things, when the chaplain is present so are the sacred things. The chaplain tries to maintain a ministry of presence throughout the service, whether in the farthest front lines or in the quiet garrison.

The ministry of presence is a concept that comes from the Christian doctrine of the Incarnation. Just as Christ became the presence of God with us in the flesh, so the chaplain becomes the presence of God in the unit. The chaplain mediates God to the soldiers in many ways. The chaplain wears the insignia of religion on the uniform, provides religious rites and sacraments, conducts public worship, and ministers with pastoral counseling. The chaplain, however, brings much more than these services to the soldier. The chaplain's mere presence in the unit carries something meaningful but very difficult to articulate.

I think, though, that every Christian knows from experience what I am talking about. I am certain that every pastor has or will experience in ministry something that happens just by being present. There is the feeling of being of service to another that does not withstand the usual tests of effectiveness and efficiency. I visited a friend who was dying. We said hello, then dropped into a deep silence. I held his hand, he responded with a squeeze. I was deeply moved by simply being present with him, and I felt no need to talk. Neither did he. I started to rehearse something to say but abandoned the effort. For twenty minutes we shared a marvelous and holy silence. He said, "Glad you came." I said, "I'm glad I came." I left feeling blessed. I felt ministered to by my dying friend, and I felt I had ministered to him.

That is ministry of presence—just being there. I have many stories of how just being there was a service to the people I was with in that moment. When I was with soldiers in combat and in tough training, I could see in their eyes that it was important to them for me to be with them. In many cases, being there became an occasion to talk about why I was there and to bring the love of Christ in more traditional language. I learned that just being there gave soldiers access to a presence that transcended my presence. There was another Presence who was at work ministering to his children through a Spirit powerful enough to use my presence for his glory. I was only a means to make Christ present.

Is that not the reason for the church's presence in the world—to make Christ present? Through public worship and acts of service, the church makes Christ real to the world. To make his real presence felt is why he ordained us to be his servants and his representatives. "It was he [Christ] who gave some to be apostles, some to be prophets, some to be evangelists, and some to be pastors and teachers, to prepare God's people for works of service, so that the body of Christ may be built up until we all reach unity of faith and in the knowledge of the Son of God and become mature, attaining to the whole measure of the fullness of Christ" (Eph. 4:11-13).

Prepare the people of God for works of service. What a noble task! We fulfill that task by being present in the world as Christ's presence. We take our stand against evil by preaching the Word, administering the sacraments, bearing the symbols, and persevering in a ministry of presence.

For Further Reflection

In his reflections on the Lord's Supper, Keizer quotes the Heidelberg Catechism to great effect. Consider Article 35 of the Belgic Confession, in which Reformed believers testify regarding this sacrament that "we do not go wrong when we say that what is eaten is Christ's own natural body and what is drunk is his own blood—but the manner in which we eat it is not by the mouth but by the Spirit, through faith."

How many members in your congregation believe in the real presence of Christ in the sacrament? What difference does this belief make in our practice of ministry?

Persevering Through Hard Times

CHAPTER 5

When the Pastor Is Broken
Leonard J. Vander Zee

Christians believe that Jesus fulfilled the wonderful words, "by his wounds we are healed" (Isa. 53:5). We can find encouragement in the Lord's words to Paul: "My grace is sufficient for you, for my power is made perfect in weakness" (2 Cor. 12:9). However, for wounded pastors to serve as wounded healers, they and their congregations must have the wisdom and courage to treat their wounds in healthy ways. In this piece, Len Vander Zee points to the power of Christian fellowship as a means of grace and healing.

The question arises with any professional caregiver: Who takes care of the doctor, the therapist, or the pastor? The answer is that in any caregiving professional's life there must be structures of care built in, as well as a healthy understanding and application of self-care. The work is too draining and the dangers too real to neglect the care of the caregiver. Yet, such neglect is all too common, not the least among pastors. In my experience, pastors have the fewest built-in care structures of any professional group. Perhaps this is one main reason for the extraordinary increase in pastoral collapse or failure. In addition to neglecting structures of care, pastors, because they preach and teach God's word, too easily begin to believe they are, or ought to be, above ordinary needs and dangers.

Who does take care of the pastor? How does the pastor know when special care is needed? Who can be trusted with this task?

I will look at these issues through an experience of care I received some years ago during a difficult time in my life. My experience was not typical by any means. It was not highly structured or even planned in advance, but, then, this was an emergency.

Not Fine at All

My wife, Judy, had been suffering with a progressively debilitating form of Multiple Sclerosis for fifteen years. When she was no longer able to care for herself due to both physical disability and severe memory loss, I made the agonizing decision, with the support of my extended family, to place her in an extended-care facility: a nursing home. It hurts even now, almost ten years later, to recall the pain of those years.

Meanwhile, I was serving a medium-sized congregation as their pastor—preaching every week, teaching, administrating, and visiting the sick, among which was now a twice-daily visit to my wife. I had already been pastor of the congregation for five years when Judy entered the nursing facility. When the congregation called me, they knew that her medical situation was precarious and that many of her worst symptoms were already evident. In their call, the congregation assured me that they were assuming responsibility for supporting me in every way with respect to my care for my wife, and they kept their word. Many members made special visits to our home when Judy still lived there. They made meals, cleaned house, or simply visited. After Judy entered the nursing facility, dozens visited her faithfully there, read to her, and prayed and sang with her. Prayer support was constant, and personal support for me was honest and appropriately probing. Members would ask, "How are you doing?" When I tossed off a smiling, "Fine," they would say, "No. I really mean: How are you doing?"

Of course, I wasn't fine at all. How can you be fine when the love of your life no longer remembers your last visit or where your children live; when you've put her in a place that's not her home? She's confused, angry, and sad—which also sums up my own feelings at the time. In addition, I was a lonely married man living a single life, which presented its own obvious dangers.

One of the skills I struggled to learn over the years of Judy's gradual decline was how to be honest in my preaching, without preaching myself rather than Christ. Obviously, a congregation will soon weary of a steady diet of the pastor's woes. Yet, my struggles could not be ignored either, without creating the proverbial 900-pound gorilla that nobody acknowledges is in the room. So, I gradually learned the art of sharing some of my personal doubts and struggles from time to time, while mixing them liberally with the big and little epiphanies of grace that God sent my way regularly. This not only gave the congregation honest preaching—I hope without an overload of my personal struggles—it also provided me with a way to work through my own painful situation with God. I knew I could not preach what I did not believe or feel. What I preached, whether it conveyed personal experience or not, had to pass a personal reality check. It also had to pass the muster of the elders, some of whom were very discerning about times when my relating of personal struggles got in the way.

As I look back to that time, and as I talk to some of the congregation members who were there, I see clearly that the congregation occasionally felt overwhelmed with how my pain and struggles were reflected in my sermons. Yet, I and others believe that some of the most effective sermons I have ever preached come from that time. Most people have an inbuilt sixth sense for pastoral phoniness and spiritual dishonesty, and they are willing to listen to less-than-positive and less-than-inspiring messages when the reality factor is evident. On the other hand, there were a few who left during that time, in part, I think, because they did not want a pastor who was struggling and who let that struggle seep into sermons. For some, I know, it brought their own doubts and struggles uncomfortably into the foreground.

At one point, soon after my wife entered the extended-care facility, I admitted to the elders that I was emotionally and spiritually burned out. The clearest signal to me was that what I was saying and doing, and what I was feeling inside, had little relationship to each other. The elders generously told me to take at least two months off with pay, and they ordered me to see a therapist, which I had already determined to do. I was away from the church completely for two months, after which, with the agreement of the elders and my therapist (and the help of some antidepressant medication) I returned. Yet, while I was now able to carry on my work with at least some energy and confidence, I was clearly still hurting.

Pastoral Care for the Pastor

It was at this time that I received the most extraordinary, scary, and healing experience of pastoral care that I had ever known. Two women in the church, one of whom was on the pastor-church relations committee, the other of whom was an elder and a therapist, came to see me. They confronted me with their penetrating understanding of the emotional and spiritual struggles I faced and with their sense that my relationship with the congregation would inevitably suffer as a result. They also made it very clear that they understood the dangers inherent in my position as a pastor who was a married man but essentially without a wife, with all the emotional and sexual deprivation that entailed. Still, they believed that I could and should continue as pastor but that I needed a different level of support and care. They proposed that I meet with them, along with their husbands, whom I also knew well and counted as my friends, every two weeks or so for an evening. The agenda would be me—my feelings, my struggles, my temptations, and my needs.

So, the five of us began to meet regularly on Sunday nights. We ate and chatted, and then they began gently and firmly to ask questions. I'm sure I was evasive at the start. Can I trust these people? If I do trust them with the dark secrets of my heart, will they be able to hear me preach the next Sunday without feeling alienated and angry? Will they continue to trust and respect me as their pastor? The answers to these questions were far from clear to me or to them. It was an experiment in the limits of honesty and care between a pastor and members of the congregation.

As time went by, trust deepened. Honesty and love triumphed over doubt and mistrust. Within a few months, I was discussing issues that I never would have dreamed I could reveal to church members—sexual fantasies and temptations, spiritual emptiness, anger with God, and inexplicable anger at my helpless wife.

One recurring issue was, of course, my loneliness and need for emotional and physical companionship. After twenty-five years of marriage, these gifts, which I had taken for granted, were simply gone. Something happened that I began to recognize only slowly over time. The two women in the group, with their husbands present, would hug me tightly before I left for the night. At first, I simply accepted and enjoyed this, but then I began to realize: This was their way of saying, "We understand you need a woman's touch and embrace, and we will give these to you in a safe environment."

My meetings with these two couples went on for many months and with varying frequency. The times we spent together were always filled with honest sharing, often punctuated with tears and bursts of anger but also with quiet, soothing conversation. They always ended in prayer. The meetings continued as my wife's condition deteriorated toward her eventual death, and our discussions involved some very difficult moral and ethical end-of-life issues that I, along with my family, needed to make.

It Takes a Congregation

As I reflect back on this extraordinary situation, I realize that I would not have taken the initiative to ask these two couples to accompany me on my journey as they did. I was often too slow to realize and address my needs. It took four people of enormous love and courage to undertake the care of their pastor. Of course, it also demanded my trust in their love and purpose.

Wouldn't it have been as useful and perhaps even better, to have this kind of relationship with a therapist or a fellow pastor? Also, many congregations have some sort of pastor-church relations committee. Wouldn't such a setting be the proper forum for this kind of care?

I certainly would not rule out the possibilities of such committees. In fact, I was involved in this and other kinds of relationships even while the unique relationship with my Sunday-night group was unfolding. However, my relationship with these four members was not therapy. It also went beyond the ordinary business of a pastor-church relations committee. It was more than a mere friendship. It was an expression of koinonia (fellowship, close relationship, communion) within the body of Christ that wrapped itself around a hurting pastor. It was the church doing its work through loving people who took the risk of honest caring. It was pastoral care in the deepest and fullest sense. It was exactly what pastors do as they journey with their members through the dark places of illness, death, temptation, and sin—except that in this case, members of the congregation were the pastors, and I was the struggling traveler, until, as I went back to my home and office and mounted the pulpit each Sunday, I was their pastor again.

Perhaps recognizing this variety of roles within a relationship is the way to grasp what seems very hard to remember: I must never see my struggling parishioners whose secrets I know, merely in terms of their problems. Instead, I can see them not only as people needing care but also as partners and peers—elders, Sunday school teachers, committee members, and members of the body of Christ with whom I work as brothers and sisters in Christ. So, too, these two couples needed to see me not only as the weeping, broken man in their living room but also as their pastor to whom they listened for God's Word each week.

I understand that my situation was in many ways unique and something that most pastors will never face. I wonder whether there should be a few people in any congregation who know their pastor in those deeply troubled times when their faith and calling are hanging by a thread—times that come to us all once or twice. Well chosen, absolutely trustworthy, and deeply committed to their pastor and their Lord, such people can provide a kind of care for a pastor that can come from nowhere else. It is *pastoral* care, which, as we all understand, is a unique relationship of profound and Christ-centered spiritual and emotional intimacy.

Remarkably, for thirteen years and up to the present—through my wife's illness, my own depression, her death, my grief, and finally my remarriage—I survived and even thrived as pastor of this congregation. I doubt many pastors have experienced such a journey in one congregation or that many congregations have sustained a relationship with their pastor through such perilous passages. Still, I can offer my story as a testimony. Through many dangers, toils, and snares, I can still enjoy a healthy relationship with this congregation, and that is a testimony to God's grace expressed through the wonderful people he called to minister to me.

For Further Reflection

Note that Vander Zee resorts to the word *koinonia* to distinguish his relationship with the two couples in his church from other relationships such as therapy, friendship, or even a pastor-church relations committee. He also defines pastoral care as "a unique relationship of profound and Christ-centered spiritual and emotional intimacy." Reflect further on the characteristics that distinguish *koinonia* or Christian fellowship from other relationships. Reflect, too, on how pastoral care and congregational relationships in general both overlap with and differ from other forms of care and relationships.

Consider also the following questions: To what extent do such distinctively Christian relationships require a distinct language? How familiar are pastors and congregations with the biblical language essential for distinctively Christian relationships? For further reflections on distinctively biblical and Christian language, pastors and congregation members may want to read *Speaking of Sin: The Lost Language of Salvation* by Barbara Brown Taylor.

CHAPTER 6

In Dependent Independence
Joel Boot

Sometimes people compare the relationship between a church and a minister to the relationship between a husband and a wife. The search process is like a courtship. The first year of ministry is like a honeymoon. A long pastorate is like a long marriage. Just as marriage includes both joys and sorrows, so does the relationship between a church and a pastor. In this piece, Joel Boot relates both the joys and sorrows of his relationships with congregations, and he shows how God proved himself faithful "for better or for worse."

It was a very hot day on October 6 in the year of our Lord 1972. The town was Le Mars, Iowa, and the church was named Calvin. I was on my knees on a rug that had been handwoven by a Christian Navajo Indian friend of my parents. My parents had sent the rug to the church as a gift, and I was kneeling on the words, somewhat crudely woven into the center: "So Send I You." I was familiar with those words, and I believed them. Little did I know what they would mean for me and my ministry. I was sent as Christ had been sent. I was called to be like Christ and to represent him to this congregation and its mission field. Yes, those were the right words on which to kneel while being ordained.

Soon, however, the staggering implications of those words began to dawn on me. I was sent by Christ, as Christ had been sent by the Father, to preach the actual Word of the Lord. I was sent to preach God's Word faithfully; compellingly; and twice, no less, each and every Sunday. I was sent to offer pastoral care to, among others, a middle-aged couple still offended by what they considered the unfair demise of my predecessor and fully prepared to see me "pay" for the "sins" that had led to his departure. I was sent, early in my ministry, to conduct the funeral of one of the founders of the church, and to discover, upon hearing of his death, that I hadn't the least idea what to do at a funeral service. I was sent to a Grizzly-Adams type by the name of Wilbur Baines who called me early one morning on my day off and told me a story that started with his growing up in the Christian Reformed Church in

Maine. I knew there was no Christian Reformed Church in Maine, but I knew that I was sent to Wilbur too. Simultaneously with all this, I became a father for the first time and realized I was sent to my daughter as well, and to her mother, my wife. Fortunately, on that warm evening in October, I did not know all this. If I had, I might have gotten off my knees and run away!

I did not run away, however, and that rug lies on the floor in front of my desk today. Its words have reminded me often that to be on my knees was the right stance not only during that ordination service but also during all the times of my service before the God who sent me. I have learned the awesome truth of what a pastor named Paul wrote to his church in Corinth:

> Such confidence as this is ours through Christ before God. Not that we are competent in ourselves to claim anything for ourselves, but our competence comes from God. He has made us competent as ministers of a new covenant—not of the letter but of the Spirit; for the letter kills, but the Spirit gives life. (2 Cor. 3:4-6)

Having had my self-confidence shaken by events in my ministry, I thank God for that moment on my knees on October 6, 1972. I thank God for the words on which I knelt and for how they remind me to place my confidence in God. I thank God for working in me and through me, and, on occasion, in spite of me. I thank him for showing me that being "competent" ["sufficient" (KJV, RSV), "qualified" (JerB, NEB, Moff.), "capable" (TEV)] is not my achievement but his gift.

Let me tell you of two events, or, better, two processes that taught me about both dependence and independence, and reminded me all the while to remain on my knees. Through these processes, I learned about providence and faith. I discovered where the rubber of the covenant hits the road of complexity. I looked deeply into the implications of church membership. I discovered the shape of love. These processes also taught me to struggle against self-righteousness while maintaining a healthy self-esteem. In these processes, I met the God before whom I knelt that October evening. I pray that, by walking along with me now, you will meet him too.

Learning Independence

Let me introduce you to a young couple whom I will call Tom and Emma (not their real names). Expecting their first child, they had moved into a duplex next door to a couple who were members of the church I served. They got to know this couple from our church, and, while they had no church affiliation of their own, they knew enough about church to know it was a place where babies were baptized. They were about to receive a newborn, and baptism seemed like a good idea to them. The only church they knew was the one to which their friends belonged, so these friends told me of their interest in baptism and asked me to call on Tom and Emma. I had mixed feelings about this. Part of me wanted to please them by simply providing what they requested, and part of me knew baptism was not so simple. I went, not so much because I wanted to, but because I knew I was being sent. They were a nice young couple with no relationship to a church and no real knowledge of God. To them, baptism was just something you did for your child as a kind of eternal life-insurance policy. I tried to explain to them that baptism was the offer of a covenant relationship with God made by God to believers and their children.

Tom and Emma simply smiled at me with the look of those trying to be polite to someone who was making no sense. However, we met again and again, and they began to understand what worship was and what church membership meant and why it was important for them to be members of the church before their child could be. They accepted my invitation to a pastor's class for prospective members. The class consisted of a dozen or so people from several different backgrounds. Some were Protestants from various denominations, some were Roman Catholics, and some had no church affiliation at all. They were there, and they were learning about the wonder of God's grace in choosing to save us. They may not have realized it, but they were going through the Canons of Dort, the Belgic Confession, and the Heidelberg Catechism. We talked of the providence of God that brought us together and of the importance of worshipping together. We experienced the "comfort," the "only comfort," of belonging, "body and soul," to God and to each other. We spoke of God's covenant faithfulness. Faith was being born in Tom and Emma, as well as in the others. After it was born, it grew. Tom and Emma were almost ready to make their public profession of faith in Jesus Christ. By this time, their baby had not only been born but was nearly two years old, and they had another child, Mary, already six months old. Tom and Emma were now looking forward not only to joining our church but also to having both their children baptized. Those baptisms would now be done with a much greater degree of understanding than would have been possible two years before. The blessed event would be all the more significant for the preparation it had entailed.

Then I received the phone call. It was one of those calls hidden deep in the words on which I had once knelt: "So Send I You." It was Tom. He and Emma were in the hospital with Mary. Would I please come?

I arrived to find Tom in the waiting room, frantically paging through a Bible story book, as if God might see him doing so and be favorably inclined toward him—and especially toward little Mary. Because of a defect in her crib, she had slipped between the mattress and the railing and had suffocated. She was now on life support in the ICU.

What could I say? How could something like this happen to such babes in faith? Why, I wondered, as they approached the kingdom, did the reception seem so hostile?

Tom was stronger than I, however, and in his own simple way, he acknowledged that Mary was God's child, not theirs, and that, come what may, she belonged to God. It was a confession of faith and a testimony all in one. In statement fashion, he answered the questions he would have been asked had he been making public profession of faith and presenting his daughter for holy baptism. His answers were followed by an urgent question: Could I please baptize Mary now?

I had an eternal, agonizing moment to decide. I realized instinctively that this was no time to be legalistic. Tom and Emma were now believers and, while we were not in church, they had surely professed their faith. Had we been in church, the very next step would have been to baptize little Mary in the threefold Name and to entrust her to the gracious care and keeping of the Almighty. Not only was baptism permissible; it was, I believed, called for. We found a little plastic container and stepped into the ICU, the three of us, and approached the tiny, naked form in the big adult bed. We asked the doctors and nurses to step back for just a moment. With water from the sink beside Mary, I touched the hot forehead of this child of the covenant and baptized her in the name of the Father and of the Son and of the Holy Spirit. Tom and Emma smiled through tears—the smile of those whose hearts were broken but who knew also they had been saved. I believe with all my heart that I had done precisely what I had been sent to do, and I say again, with pastor Paul, and with even greater confidence than before: "He has made us competent as ministers of a new covenant—not of the letter but of the Spirit; for the letter kills, but the Spirit gives life" (2 Cor. 3:6).

The "letter" that day would have killed, just as surely as the broken crib had, but the Spirit offered "life." Mary's little heart stopped the next afternoon. Her parents' hearts broke, but their faith lived and grew, and they did join our church and God's kingdom. I thank God for this experience and for all it taught me about providence and faith and covenant and faithfulness and what it means to be church. I also thank God most of all for helping me to distinguish between "letter" and "Spirit" so I could act as a minister of the latter. "Such confidence as this is ours through Christ before God." I was learning independence in dependence on my heavenly Father.

Learning Dependence

Some years later, I was called to another church in another place. I had never allowed myself even to think of serving in such a church and place. At the time, this was one of the largest congregations in the Christian Reformed denomination, and when the position of senior pastor there was declared open, a friend of mine told me he thought I had the gifts for that position and ought to apply. I did not apply. Instead, I told myself that if God wanted me there, God would call me there.

Not long after, a letter came, inviting my participation in the search process for this position—pastor of preaching in one of the Christian Reformed Church's premier pulpits. I was stunned! I was honored! I was afraid! But something—Someone?—inside me told me to cooperate. So I did. I answered pages of questions and endured hours of interviews. Finally, the church narrowed its search to me and one other minister. When I asked who the other candidate was, I was given the name of someone known denomination-wide, and I secretly felt I had been included simply to make the search look balanced. I was sure he would be called, and I would stay where I was. I remember spending time on my knees during the whole process but then dropping to my knees in frightened apprehension when I was told I had been overwhelmingly selected to receive the call. While the process took much longer than I have time to describe, I concluded and still believe with all my heart that this call was from God himself, and I had no choice but to accept it. So, within six months of the retirement of my predecessor who had been there for nearly four decades, I prepared to assume this pulpit, which was the envy of many.

The congregation had more than its fair share of college professors and college-educated professionals, and I found this more than mildly intimidating. One of them, who had taught me freshman English nearly twenty years before, called me long distance and informed me that if I became his pastor, well, he'd be my pastor. I could talk with him, he said, about anything or anyone in the strictest confidence. He would be there, he promised, to let God use him to give me strength. Little did I know not only how grateful I would be for that offer but how much and how often I would take him up on it. For several years, until his untimely death, this professor ministered to me at a weekly coffee or lunch date and kept his wonderful promise. I marvel, in retrospect, at the wisdom of God in calling such a one to be my pastor while calling me to be his. He was another way, another person, through whom God himself was providing the "competence" he had promised for ministry.

Over the years, this congregation had, largely without its knowledge, assumed a certain personality, and it was tempted to think more highly of itself than it should have. My call to this high place prompted the same temptation in me. I even acknowledged to this congregation that I often felt like Nebuchadnezzar surveying this great city which, if I had not built, I had at least inherited. These two personalities, the church's and mine, inevitably and painfully clashed.

I was not my predecessor. I was not trying to be different; I was just being myself, but I was different, very different, from the pastor who had led this congregation for many years. Some in the congregation assumed that the way it had always been was the way it was always supposed to be. Things such as children coming to the front of the sanctuary for children's messages irked some. My sermon outlines were critiqued grammatically, not theologically. I was told I looked too relaxed when I crossed my legs while seated on the pulpit chair. When our daughter made profession of faith and I kissed her cheek, I was criticized for that. I was told repeatedly and in a variety of ways that my sermons lacked depth—they were soup and not meat. While I suspect that few, if any, of my detractors meant it exactly in this way, the Devil saw to it that these criticisms ate away at my confidence in what up until then I had considered my greatest gifts—my leadership in worship and preaching. At the pinnacle of my career, I came closer to resignation than at any other time during my, thus far, thirty years of ministry. Not only did I fall for Nebuchadnezzar's temptation to consider myself far more important than I should have, I also felt I was being punished like Nebuchadnezzar and forced out to pasture before my time. I became defensive. I grew depressed. I felt angry. Finally, I was broken.

I realized later that I, like Elijah before me, was suffering from a form of myopia. All I saw was the pain. All I knew was the fear. I developed a kind of I-only-I-am-left-and-they-seek-my-life-to-take-it-away complex and often failed to see the presence of God in the host of kind and supportive parishioners who stood by my side, not so much defending me as a person, but serving and worshipping God along with me. Like the seven thousand in Israel whom Elijah had failed to see, I often lost sight of these supporters. This remains another important lesson God taught me—to keep my eyes fixed on him. To fix them anywhere else is not only to lose confidence but to lose competence.

I did not realize it immediately, but eventually I saw that God was not inflicting the pain but, rather, was using it for my healing. God was not inspiring the fear but, instead, was channeling it toward my well-being. God was not breaking me, but God did need me to be broken. Then, in pieces at his feet, I found myself not only older and wiser but also on my knees again and back on that rug where it had all begun. There, listening to his voice—not my own, and not any others'—I heard God speaking through pastor Paul once more and learning from him:

> To keep me from becoming conceited . . . there was given me a thorn in my flesh, a messenger of Satan, to torment me. Three times I pleaded with the Lord to take it away from me. But he said to me, "My grace is sufficient for you, for my power is made perfect in weakness." Therefore I will boast all the more gladly about my weaknesses, so that Christ's power may rest on me. That is why, for Christ's sake, I delight in weaknesses, in insults, in hardships, in persecutions, in difficulties. For when I am weak, then I am strong. (2 Cor. 12:7-10)

This process made no earthly sense, but it was the way of the kingdom. I was broken into wholeness, weakened into strength, and humiliated into humility. Today, I thank God for this valley, for it was in the valley that I had no choice but to look up. It was when I felt I could no longer stand that I found myself back on my knees where I belonged. In dependence is where I once again found my independence. In that respect, I, like Paul, "delight in" my "weaknesses."

Lessons to Be Shared

I no longer serve that church. Perhaps you are wondering how and when and whether you may or must leave a particular situation. There are, of course, no ironclad rules of procedure. Perhaps I can simply relate what happened to me. I wanted to leave; I truly wanted to leave often. I concluded, however, that what I wanted and what God wanted were not one and the same thing. There were challenges in my current charge to be met, tasks to be fulfilled, and loose ends to be tied up. It became apparent to me, through much prayer and conversation, that there were things to finish before I could be finished.

So I waited; and, while I waited, I worked; and while I worked, I watched; and when the responsibilities of that charge were fulfilled, God made that clear through another church's contact with me, not mine with it. I not only concluded that I could go, but, much more satisfying, I concluded that God was saying to me, "Go." Once again, it was through dependence that I gained a sense of independence.

I have learned through these experiences that this is where pastoral independence is to be found—in dependence. When I began my ministry, I did so on my knees. You probably began there too. I urge you to assume that position often. Whether figuratively or literally on your knees before God, depend on him. That day in the ICU of Oakwood Hospital I stood on my feet but ministered on my knees. There is no textbook for such situations. The goal is to possess the "confidence" that "is ours through Christ before

God." It is in that confidence that we can truly minister. It is when we yield ourselves to him and let him use us that we are truly useful. It is when we recognize that "our competence comes from God" that we are finally beginning to be competent.

During dark days at another place later on in my ministry, I began to sense that I had lost sight of that key. I had put my confidence in myself. I had assumed my own competence. I had to learn that I could not stand on my own. God used hurts to heal. God used broken pieces to make me whole. God used weakness to lead me to strength. God used fear and anxiety and loneliness to remind me that we are not "competent in ourselves to claim anything for ourselves, but our competence comes from God." True independence, the ability to stand, comes from living on one's knees—in dependence on the God from whom alone any competence comes.

For Further Reflection

Compare Joel Boot's story of baptism with Kathy Smith's story of baptism and Herm Keizer's stories about the Lord's Supper earlier in this book. How did each pastor respect the church's understanding of the sacraments while following the Spirit who gives life?

Boot notes that there is no ironclad procedure for pastors to follow in deciding "how and when and whether" to leave a particular position. What light does his narrative shed with respect to discerning the Spirit's leading in this regard? What role should the council, church visitors, and others play as pastors try to discern whether to stay or go?

CHAPTER 7

Restoring a Lapsed Member and Pastor
Pedro Aviles

In this piece, Pedro Aviles puts flesh and blood on the word pastor. *He reflects on what it means to be both a good shepherd and, at the same time, a lost sheep. He calls attention to the role of discipline in the life of the church and witnesses to the suffering and the glory of life under the authority of "the Chief Shepherd." (See 1 Peter 5:1-11.)*

I sit in a circle surrounded by the elders and deacons of my church. In this disciplinary meeting, I am the one undergoing the process of discipline. My senior pastor-mentor is upset with my stubborn indifference and rebellion. If I don't repent, I will be excommunicated.

How did I get to this point? Here I am, twenty-six years old, with a young wife who loves me, part of a dynamic inner-city ethnic church, and surrounded by leaders who love me. Why am I giving up on the church and God?

A year ago, I was commissioned by my home church to plant a new church as a "tentmaker." My wife and I moved into the targeted community and began to familiarize ourselves with our neighbors. However, our efforts never seemed to go beyond that. She and I still had to work our full-time jobs—hers during the day and mine during the evenings. In addition, we still had ministry responsibilities in our home church.

As months went by, I could not establish a new believes' Bible study. The pressure to see results began to create tension between my wife and me. In addition to this, I was inconsistent in my personal walk with God. I struggled with the lust of my eyes as I found them wandering where they ought not to go.

On top of guilt, I felt shame about failing in my mission to plant a church, and this was more than I felt I could handle. I stopped caring about the ministry, my marriage, and my God. So without telling anyone, not even my wife, I determined to run. Like Jonah fleeing from God in a ship, I joined the Navy and was assigned to leave for boot camp in three months.

A week after I enlisted, I told my wife. She called the pastor of our home church, and now I sit in this meeting. The pastor and elders try to exhort me to return to my first love, God, and to my wife. I do not listen and tell them that whatever they say won't matter because I will join the Navy anyway. With tears and much love, they urge me to return to God; I refuse. They tell me that at the next Sunday service they will inform the church of my situation. Then they pray for me, and I quietly leave that sad room.

For the next two months I did not go to church. Tension with my wife continued. A few times a church leader called to see how I was doing, but I didn't respond. The only one I could not completely shut out was God. I enjoyed Christian contemporary music and still listened to it even when I did not read my Bible or pray. Through the music, God kept speaking to me until he convinced me that he loved and forgave me and was willing to help me start anew.

A month before my departure, I cried and told my wife and pastor how sorry I was. I desperately wanted to be restored to an obedient relationship to God and to the church. I met again with all the church leaders and confessed my rebellion and asked for their forgiveness and support in helping me live an obedient life. They cried and rejoiced with me. The following Sunday morning, I went to church, and they announced my return to God. They loved and forgave me and embraced me back into their community.

I felt it was the sheer goodness of a loving God that restored me. God worked grace upon grace. My pastor and I wrote letters to the Navy recruiting officers explaining my situation and my condition at the time I joined. A week before I was to be shipped off to boot camp, I got a letter from the Navy dismissing my commitment to them. God is truly good.

Thirty Years Later

Years later, I again passed through a time when the weight of pastoring the church seemed unbearable. Somehow I had thought that after all my seminary training I would be able to handle whatever came my way. I was wrong. Once again, I felt severe pressures in the church and building tension in my marriage. My wife and I got into another argument about the ministry. It went like this.

A Wife Speaks Truth

Urging me to action, Diana demanded, "You have to visit him and talk to him about his lack of tithing." She paused. "And while you're at it, find out why he hasn't been coming to the last few Sunday services; O.K.?" My wife is the church treasurer and my administrative assistant.

Immediately my defenses went up. I don't like it when she starts telling me what to do, as though I weren't aware of my pastoral responsibilities. As she waited for a response, in my mind I thought, *I already have a hundred-and-one urgent things to do. Can't I just let go of this one thing for a while longer?* She placed her fists on her hips and gave me an impatient stare.

Exasperated, I threw up my hands and said, "O.K., O.K., I'll call one of the elders to follow up and make a visit. They can see what's up."

"No you don't," she responded, recognizing my attempt to evade responsibility. "You're the pastor, and the people need to see that you care for them."

It seemed that she believed it was my responsibility to follow up on all members who were absent for a while and/or had ceased to tithe faithfully to our church. I wondered if she thought this was the only task in my ministry. I also wondered if my priorities were upside down.

My ministry includes the preparation of two sermons per week; a weekly lesson for my home Bible study; counseling a few marriages that are crumbling; making weekly hospital visits; going to a small weekly prayer meeting; and administering the elders, deacons, worship team, youth pastor, and teachers of the Sunday school classes. I also chair both the local Christian school board and the new building program in the church in addition to continuing my postgraduate courses. I'm sure I'm forgetting something here. Oh yes, I have to care for my wife and my children, plus keep up with my devotional life. My priorities definitely are upside down.

I know that the shepherd (pastor) is called to seek the lost sheep. I have to admit, though, that I don't like the "discipline" part of the pastorate—that part when I have to visit a wayward person who, as a result of his own doing, makes a mess of his life that I have to help clean up.

I know I preach and teach well. At least that is what the people say when they fill out the weekly sermon evaluation forms. I'd gladly bear the responsibility of discipleship training, teaching, preaching, and leading worship and Bible studies. However, as to visitation and following up on lapsed members and disciplining members in sin—that I'd rather do without.

Snapping her fingers in my eyes, my wife pulled me away from my thoughts saying, "Are you listening to me?" I wasn't. "Well, just in case you weren't. I'll say one last thing. Remember the lesson you said you learned from Jesus about how the shepherd breaks his wandering sheep's leg. Remember!"

A Shepherd Breaks the Sheep's Leg

How can I forget that story? I don't remember where I first heard it. However, it had moved me deeply.

From Jesus' parable in Luke 15:4-7, it is obvious that a shepherd will go after his lost sheep and bring that sheep back into the fold. However, if a particular sheep keeps wandering from the herd and will not heed the shepherd's voice, the shepherd will eventually seek out that sheep and intentionally break one of its legs. Then, with tenderness, he will mend that leg. He will carry that sheep on his shoulder for the weeks it takes for the leg to heal. In the meantime, the shepherd will lovingly care for and feed the sheep from his own hands. Because of the discipline of the broken leg and all the love the shepherd gives, the result is that the sheep no longer wanders from the shepherd. The sheep now loves the shepherd and listens to his voice.

Why did my wife want me to remember this story? Early in my ministry I had an antagonistic church member who intimidated me. I avoided confronting him, and I agonized in prayer about what to do. One day as I prayed, I heard Jesus, my Good Shepherd, speak in my heart. He said, "You must go and break that sheep's leg." Without a doubt, I knew it was my responsibility to bring correction to this person. However, I still had some fears about obeying my shepherd's voice. While still praying, Father God, the Great Shepherd (Heb. 12:5-11; 13:20), made sure I understood the seriousness of my pastoral responsibility by speaking these words to me, "If you don't do this, I will break your leg." I cried in repentance regarding my hesitation to do his will. The choice was either I break that rebellious sheep's leg (correcting the church member) or God breaks my leg (correcting me). In the weeks that followed, I spoke many times with this person who needed correction.

A Church Board Struggles with Restoration

What my wife did not know was that two weeks earlier at the monthly board meeting with the elders and deacons, I had shared how overwhelmed I felt with the burdens of ministry. Furthermore, I shared my frustration with some church members on whom I depended but who were unfaithful in attending the Sunday services. The elders and deacons began asking many questions regarding what might be happening to these lapsed members.

Elder Bob wanted clarity and asked, "Are we talking about taking some disciplinary measures against those church members who might be in sin?"

The newest deacon to the church board, Ray, asked, "Does an effective method exist to restore members who are disengaging from the life of the church?"

One of the veteran deacons of five years, Joe, said, "If one exists, it is too lenient with people in sin. We must follow up on these lapsed members right away and exhort them to repent of their sins."

Elder Susanna, the first woman elder of the church, rejected Joe's statement and said; "We are too quick to pass judgment on people before we have all the facts. Besides it is easier to catch bees with honey. Let's be careful."

As chairman, I allowed them to debate this for a little while. I felt they needed time to express their opinions and feelings. Finally, deacon Ray asked me directly, "Pastor, tell us your thoughts and what should be done with these lapsed members."

I said, "It seems to me that in most cases I, as pastor, must be involved somehow in pursuing this member." I could tell he wanted more.

Deacon Ray persisted, "But what steps do we have in place that can detail or outline the process of restoring alienated, disgruntled, and apathetic members?"

I scanned the other faces around the table and could read concern and a willingness to support my suggestions. This was a good group of leaders. So I said, "Before I answer that or look at the denominational handbook on church governance, let's look at some passages in the Bible. You leaders analyze them and give a brief report of your findings." The passages were Exodus 18, Matthew 18:15-20, Acts 6:1-7, and Galatians 6:1-10.

Actually, I didn't want to say what I thought. It seemed better if they developed their own working knowledge of the Scriptures. I divided them into groups of three and gave each group one of the passages. Their assignment was to take ten minutes to identify the practical steps toward restoration, to identify who is to do what in that process, and finally, to pinpoint when I, as pastor, should step in.

Those ten minutes turned into more than thirty. I allowed them to take as much time as they needed, knowing that as they struggled with creating this process, they would have greater ownership of it. My hope was to have the elders see with greater clarity the importance of their ministry role. I also hoped (and this is where I may have been self-seeking) that my part in the restoration process would not be at the beginning but at the end, after the elders had done their part. In this way, I might not even be needed if a lapsed member responded positively to the elders.

During this process, I recognized again my struggle with visitation and follow-up. I wondered if I even had a calling and gift for the traditional pastoral role. I love the encouraging and equipping part of ministry. However, I have little desire to visit people. What does that say about my giftedness to pastor?

The meeting was profitable. The elders and deacons developed the entire restoration process; I simply facilitated. This greatly pleased me because the church now had a healthy method of follow-up that places the elders in the forefront. Discipline was no longer a subjective matter determined by me, the pastor. It was the work of many leaders within the congregational body. (The guidelines for restoration of lapsed members are found at the end of this chapter.)

Restoring a Lapsed Pastor

After our lengthy discussion, we had about fifteen minutes left in our board meeting and many more agenda points to cover. While I looked over the agenda, wondering what I could postpone, I casually asked, "Is there anything else regarding restoration, that we have not addressed?" I did not expect any response. However, I was surprised when elder Sam asked for a moment to speak.

Elder Sam was a tall white-haired man with deep gray eyes. The oldest member of the board, he seldom spoke, but when he did, he displayed great insight and wisdom. My attention was on the agenda, so he asked me to focus on his words. I could see and feel him looking directly into my eyes as though he were reading the condition of my soul.

He spoke in a deliberate pace, "Pastor, people in the church won't care how much you know, until they know how much you care." There was total silence in the room. As Sam said this, I could feel the presence of God increasing in the room.

He proceeded to say, "Pastor, you are a knowledgeable and gifted teacher. At my age, I've heard many ministers, and I know. Your expository preaching is of high quality. But, pastor, if you want the support of your people, you must love them deeply and instruct them simply."

His words felt like a surgeon's knife. They cut open my chest and revealed my indifferent heart. At that point, I began to feel a lump of sorrow welling up in my throat and tears forming in my eyes. In silence, I found myself moving my head up and down slightly, affirming his words.

With gentle firmness he said, "Pastor, I love you. You can count on me to stand with you in good times and bad. But I wonder: Will you do the same for me? If I get sick, will you visit me?" He paused. "Will you come because it is your duty or because you love me?"

I wanted to say yes, yes, but nothing came out. I was exposed. I was receiving loving correction.

Elder Sam, the spiritual surgeon, skillfully spoke words that cut away at the spiritual tumor in my heart. He said, "God calls you pastor, and that's what you are to me. I can see right now that something of God's Spirit is stirring in your heart. I feel led to read some words Jesus spoke to another man in the Bible."

He took out his old well-worn Bible and read these words, "Again, Jesus said, 'Simon son of John, do you truly love me?' He answered, 'Yes Lord, you know that I love you.' Jesus said, 'Take care of my sheep'" (John 21:16).

Now, I am broken, and I can barely keep myself from crying out loud.

Elder Sam asks all the elders and deacons to gather around me so they could pray for me. As they laid hands on me and prayed, the floodgates opened wide, and I cried and cried while asking God to forgive me. I couldn't hear what they were praying because all of them were praying aloud at the same time. All I felt was compassion and loving correction.

My shepherd God had turned the tables on me again. Now, I was the one being corrected. I was the lost sheep being restored. I felt the power of God's Spirit changing my heart and giving me a love for his people, even for the ones who leave the church.

Back to a Wife Who Speaks Truth

The events of this board meeting had taken place two weeks before my wife confronted me. I had not told her what had happened, and I had quickly reverted to my old patterns. Now, again, I was arguing with my wife about how I was too busy to do any visits. However, in a flash, God's Spirit brought to my mind those words of "breaking the sheep's leg." I recalled the statement my wife had made, "You're the pastor and the people need to see that you care for them." Again the Spirit reminded me of what had transpired in that board meeting and of Sam's Spirit-led words.

For the first time, I shared with my wife the details of that night and how God had touched me. I confessed to her, "You are right, and I am sorry for my indifference. I promise to call and follow up. I will also call the elders, so together we can pursue the restoration process." She was satisfied.

She left me alone for a while. I prayed, "Good Shepherd Jesus, help me to love your people and to pursue them as you pursued me."

Process of Restoring a Lapsed Member

Below are the steps my church board members plan to use to restore a lapsed member. Note: Two people are to go together to make these visits. One of the two must be an elder. Also, a week or two may pass between the steps.

Step 1 - First Visit

The goal here is to demonstrate love and concern for the lapsed member, not to judge or criticize. The elders believe this visit should focus on showing a deep concern for the spiritual well being of the member. Why? Because they believe that the absence of the lapsed member can be a symptom of a deeper issue. No one as yet knows what is truly happening in the life of this member; there might be some legitimate reason for the lapse.

If the member has any issues against the church, the elders are to seek a proper resolution with the appropriate parties in a timely manner. At the end of the meeting, the elders are to pray for the member and invite him back to fellowship in the church. Again, attendance is not to be emphasized.

If the member responds positively to this visit by the elders, we all rejoice and embrace this member back into church life.

Step 2 - Second Visit

If this member does not respond positively to the elders' first visit or he does not start attending the worship services, then a second visit is necessary. The goal is still to demonstrate love and concern for the spiritual welfare of the lapsed member. Questions can be asked about the member's moral-spiritual life, but the elders are not to judge or criticize—only encourage and support. At the end of the meeting, the elders are to pray for the member and invite him to church.

If the member responds positively to this visit by the elders, we all rejoice and embrace this member back into church life.

Step 3 - Pastor Visits

If this member does not respond positively to the elders' second visit, and he still does not attend the worship services, then a third visit is necessary. The pastor must be involved in this third visit. The goal is still to love and show concern. However, the lapsed member will be asked directly to explain where his relationship and commitment stand with God and with the church. The pastor and elders at this point are seeking clear signs of repentance (that is, change of thinking about God and the church [Matt. 8:8]). A definite answer of commitment to Christ and the local church is sought here.

If the member responds positively to this visit by the elders, we all rejoice and embrace this member back into church life.

Step 4 - Lapsed Member Removed

However, if, after some urging, it is clear that the lapsed member does not want to remain committed to Christ and the church, then, based on his decision, the outcome will be that at the next members' meeting he will be removed from membership. This unrepentant member is told this and is asked if that is what he wants. If he says yes, then at the end of this visit, the elders are to pray for him and commit him to God's hands (Heb. 12).

In this final step, at the very next members meeting, all the members are publicly informed about the moral-spiritual condition of the lapsed member, the process followed by the elders and pastor to restore him, and the lapsed member's decision to leave the church community. All the people at the meeting are encouraged to follow up with the lapsed member if they feel so led. In the meantime, the lapsed member is removed from church membership. Prayers will be offered on behalf of the lapsed member in the hope that even this step of discipline will eventually lead finally to restoration.

For Further Reflection
Read the story of Jesus' restoration of Peter in John 21:15-19. Spend some time in prayer and see if the Spirit brings the names of any congregational sheep to your mind.

Article 29 of the Belgic Confession lists the practice of church discipline as one of the marks of the true church. How does the practice of discipline in your congregation compare with the biblical passages that Rev. Pedro Aviles gave his elders to study? What guidance do the confessions and the Church Order offer? Would you agree with those who say that the key to church discipline is the practice of discipleship?

What steps in the restoration plan that Pastor Aviles supplies would transfer fittingly to your congregation? What steps would have to be revised in your context?

Running the Race with Joy

CHAPTER 8

Our "Kamikaze" Sailing Adventure
Richard E. Sytsma

Acts 2 portrays the pouring out of the Holy Spirit in such a compelling way that sometimes believers forget the story of the Spirit, and the church continues for twenty-six more chapters and beyond. In this piece, Rich Sytsma shows that the Spirit of Pentecost blows not only in swift and dramatic ways but also in steady and quiet ways. Perhaps after reflecting on Sytsma's extended use of the sailing metaphor, believers in all kinds of settings will learn to say of their various ministry plans that they "seemed good to the Holy Spirit and to us" (Acts 15:28).

For thirty-two years Sandy and I survived and, yes, even thrived as missionaries in Japan. We did not see rapid church growth. We encountered obstacles to the gospel at every turn. We desperately wanted the Japanese to understand and respond to God's love, yet few actually did. Nevertheless we can also honestly say that God blessed our ministry. We witnessed heartwarming conversions and saw churches grow from nothing to become self-supporting congregations. We became so much a part of the Japanese church that when we left, we left a big part of ourselves behind. We left Japanese brothers and sisters who were deeply saddened to say good-bye to us. Sensing God's blessing on us and his blessing others through us was both humbling and gratifying.

Our ministry in Japan began in October 1968 when Sandy and I sailed from San Francisco on the *President Cleveland* bound for Yokohama. *Sailed* may not be the most accurate word to describe our trip across the Pacific Ocean. That huge ocean liner had no sails, and, until toward the end of the trip when we nearly intersected the path of a typhoon, we were oblivious to the wind. Sailing, however, is an apt metaphor for our adventure with God in ministry.

It has been the gracious wind of God's Spirit that kept us going the past thirty-six years. As I review those years, I can identify a few ways in which God's Spirit carried us on—sometimes with a gentle breeze, sometimes with amazing force. Or to put it another way, I can identify a few guidelines that helped us catch the divine wind and sail God's ship forward.

Setting Sail—Following the Call

The confidence that God had called Sandy and me to minister in Japan continually sustained us in that ministry. God's call to us to go to Japan was so clear. We knew we were sailing in the right direction. Already in high school, I had felt called to enter the ministry. People around me told me I had gifts for ministry, and they echoed what I was feeling in my heart. Later, I came to see that God used my childhood experiences as an MK, missionary kid, in Japan to prepare me for ministry in that land.

After I was graduated from seminary, God gave us a wonderful opportunity to serve under Christian Reformed Home Missions on loan to Inter-Varsity Christian Fellowship in San Jose, California. He used the 1967 Urbana Missions Convention to make me realize that it was ministry in Japan for which I was training.

At Urbana, Rev. Akira Hatori, a well-known Japanese radio minister, challenged all of us with the spiritual need in Japan, a country where 99.5 per cent of the people were living in spiritual darkness. He pleaded with us to help reach the Japanese for Christ. As he talked, I felt God's pulling on my heartstrings. Before that I had often thought about missionary service in Japan. As an MK who had lived in Japan since I was ten, I had developed a love for Japan and its people. The example of my parents and other missionaries who had been serving faithfully as church planters had inspired me. I knew firsthand how immense the spiritual vacuum was in Japan, and I had seen how God's love had filled that vacuum when the Japanese put their faith in Christ. So, when Rev. Akira Hatori pleaded, "Come to Japan," I heard those words as a confirmation of God's call. Sandy, who as a girl had dreamed of becoming a missionary, was also willing. For more than thirty years, the assurance that we were where God wanted us to be sustained us in Japan.

Catching the Divine Wind—Staying Close to God and Appropriating His Power

Sailing is all about catching the wind. In our case, it was about catching the divine wind. (The Japanese word *kamikaze* literally means "divine wind.") The longer I am engaged in ministry the more I realize that the integrity and vibrancy of my ministry is intimately tied to my maintaining a close relationship with God. If I neglect my routine of personal and family devotions, if worship becomes perfunctory, or if sin remains unconfessed, my inner resources for doing God's work dry up and my ministry loses its effectiveness.

For me, the key to staying intimate with God through personal devotions and family devotions is building these quiet times into the rhythm of life so that that they become habits. A daily routine of personal prayer and Bible reading has been hard for me to maintain in a life that routinely had little routine, but I have kept coming back to its importance.

Family devotions are an even higher priority. We try to plan evening mealtimes so that we are able to pray and read the Bible. When the children were young, we prayed with them at bedtime. When the kids reached high school age, I taught them the Heidelberg Catechism. Our children are appreciative of our efforts to teach and model the faith, but they tell us now that they wish we had been more intentional about teaching them Reformed doctrine.

Another priority was Sunday worship as a family in a Japanese church. Although worshipping in Japanese was difficult at times, it proved to be immensely rewarding for our whole family. We and our missionary colleagues also nurtured our families in the faith by holding annual mission retreats and monthly mission worship services in English on Sunday afternoons. How we loved to sing the familiar hymns from the Psalter Hymnal. Annual vacations were another "must." To keep going, we needed to retreat a little while, tie up our family boat, and give it a rest. Vacations were absolutely necessary, and they were positively wonderful for family health. Our family still looks with nostalgia at those special times we enjoyed at a missionary vacation spot in the mountains.

Weekly highlights in our prayer life were the midweek prayer meetings in the churches we served. What open sharing and honest praying took place in those little gatherings. Christians prayed for the salvation of their family members. Our brothers and sisters sometimes shed tears as they confessed their sins and pleaded with God to heal broken relationships. Seekers honestly poured out their doubts and hopes to God. At times, they asked God for forgiveness for the first time in their lives in these small-group settings. We were amazed by how free the Japanese felt to share and pray about very personal matters. How I miss those simple midweek prayer meetings. These prayer gatherings were sails that caught the Spirit's breezes and pulled the little ecclesiastical "ship" along.

Learning the Ropes—Continuing Education

Sailing requires more than simply hoisting the sail. It requires learning the ropes and how to respond to changes in the wind. In our mission work, we had to learn the ropes as well. Communicating with sophisticated, educated Japanese people requires a high level of academic training. Presenting the gospel to people who think of "god" as anything that inspires awe and who define "sin" as "crime" demands careful thought and imagination. I needed all the theological training I received at Calvin Seminary, but I also needed to learn much more. As missionary colleague Dr. Harvey Smit said to us, "You will learn more here than you teach. The field makes the missionary, not the other way around. It takes humility to be a missionary."

Our language study proved to be a lesson in humility. For two years, we studied the Japanese language on a full-time basis. My original goal was to master Japanese completely—to speak, read, and write the language the way the Japanese do. I did well in the language, but never reached that level of fluency. Even though I am a perfectionist, this did not bother me. As I saw how God used other missionaries, it soon became obvious that language fluency was not the most important key in ministry. It was love. "If I speak in the tongues of men and of angels, but have not love, I am a resounding gong or clanging cymbal." Sometimes the notes I sounded in the Japanese language were quite gonglike simply because my language skills were deficient, so language acquisition was important. However, this skill was not nearly as important as being filled with God's love. My prayer for language study became a prayer not that I would sound perfect, but that I could communicate God's love.

Sermon preparation involved moving from the original biblical languages and context, through my own English/American thought forms, and then into the Japanese language and cultural context. The task became easier as the years passed, but it was always a challenge. At first I wrote my sermons in Japanese, but that tied me too closely to the manuscript and made for poor eye contact. So I settled on another strategy: using an English manuscript, I simultaneously translated it into Japanese. With this approach I made more grammatical mistakes, but I had a freer delivery and better eye contact.

We needed to be prepared to "preach" at all times. God gave us opportunities to share the gospel on the street, on trains, in supermarkets, at schools, and in hospitals. Once I received an unexpected opportunity to share the gospel with my doctor. After performing an angioplasty procedure on me, he wheeled me to another part of the operating room, where he stood over me and put pressure on the incision where he had inserted the catheter. He had to do this for about thirty to forty minutes so the incision would close up. During this time, I was lying stark naked, and he was applying pressure to my groin. He chose that moment to say, "I don't know anything about Christianity. Could you tell me what it is all about?" So, dressed in my birthday suit, I preached the gospel to my doctor. As the apostle Peter said, "Always be prepared to give an answer to everyone who asks you to give the reason for the hope that you have." The biggest part of our being prepared is what Peter says in the first part of this verse: "But in your hearts set apart Christ as Lord." Following Christ as Lord means that evangelism takes incarnational form. We live God's grace and truth so that, when we talk about God's grace and truth, our words ring true.

Learning the ropes includes continuing education, which, in my case took place during our times of home service. My first two furloughs were spent in Ann Arbor, where I studied Japanese language, literature, history, and religion at the University of Michigan Graduate School. During the third study furlough, I took missiology courses at Calvin Seminary. In Tokyo, Sandy did some continued study in Japanese language, art, and religion at Sophia University, and we both attended numerous seminars, retreats, and conferences for missionaries.

This study was invaluable, but it entailed sacrifice. The two years of Japanese language study was manageable because, besides teaching two English Bible classes a week, I had no other responsibilities during that time. The study in the States on home service was another matter. I studied during the week and preached and did deputation on weekends. In Ann Arbor, we lived on a street named Cram Place, and that was a fitting address because I crammed eight or nine days' worth of activities into seven. I had very little time for the family, and, of course, we enjoyed no Sabbath rest. Furloughs were always stressful and unsettled times, but study furloughs were extra stressful. At the time, I experienced no adverse health effects, but it is very possible that this stress contributed to the heart attack I experienced at age 51. If I could do it over again, I would still opt for continuing education, but I would be more realistic about how much I could cram into a week.

Sailing Together—Mission Teamwork

I did not sail alone in my mission adventure. I was part of a team of sailors, and it was important that we worked together. The popular stereotype of the missionary as an independent-minded "lone-ranger" did not at all fit us. Our spouses, Japanese co-workers, fellow missionaries, and members of the congregations were colleagues without whom we could not have functioned. Supporting these collegial relationships were networks of larger partnerships: the Christian Reformed Church in North America-Reformed Church in Japan (CRCNA-RCJ) ecclesiastical ties, the field home-office teamwork, and the bonds between missionaries and supporting churches.

Sandy was my closest partner—my missionary colleague in fact if not always in name. Although she was not ordained or paid as a missionary, she served as a missionary just as much as I did. The work we did, we did together. As language students, we studied together. As church planters, we scouted new church planting sites together. We also planned worship services together. I preached, taught Bible classes, and trained church leaders. Sandy played the organ, taught Sunday school as well as ladies' Bible and English classes, and networked in the neighborhood. When I was given the task of field director, I organized the mission, and Sandy organized the mission office and showed hospitality to the steady stream of visitors we received. Sandy's friendly demeanor, ability to adapt well to Japanese rules of decorum, and her gifts of hospitality and teaching made her a very effective missionary. It has been a privilege to be her teammate.

My second most important partnership was my working relationship with Japanese co-workers. In the twenty-eight years I served as church planter, I served seven emerging churches. In each church, I worked alongside a Japanese pastor, or to put it more accurately, Sandy and I teamed up with a Japanese pastor and his wife. Typically, the pastor lived with his family in a parsonage attached to the sanctuary and was recognized as "the pastor" of the emerging congregation. I worked with the pastor until the emerging group reached organizational maturity, and then I left to begin a new church plant with another pastor. As pastor and missionary, we shared the preaching and teaching responsibilities. The pastor carried the lion's share of the pastoral load, led steering-committee meetings and congregational meetings and in general functioned as the pastor. With our native English-speaking ability and Caucasian features, Sandy and I were able to attract newcomers and build relationships with them.

In these missionary-pastor partnerships I learned very early the importance of being honest and frank with each other in private and showing a unified "face" to the church. That meant that the two of us always met together to talk things over, work out differences, and pray before we met with the steering committee or congregation. Also, all missionaries and Japanese pastors gathered three times a year for fellowship, discussion of issues and mission strategies, and training. These "Inter Nos" ("among ourselves") meetings helped missionaries and pastors to keep the lines of communication open and provided significant continuing-education opportunities.

Collegiality marked our relationships with other missionaries as well. Our fellow missionaries were our co-workers and our surrogate family. We needed and stimulated each other. The Japanese group cultural trait of making decisions by consensus was highly ingrained in our mission field. We alternated strategy meetings and business meetings. In our strategy meetings, we made no formal decisions but informally worked on gaining consensus on important issues coming up, so very seldom were there close votes in our business meetings. Because decisions affected not only our work but also where we lived and where our children attended school, gaining consensus was essential to a smoothly functioning mission. Over the years, the mission-field structure vacillated between democratic and hierarchical models, but no matter what the organizational charts looked like, we operated in collegial fashion. We sailed together.

Sailing through the Storm—Facing Conflict

The course of our mission voyage took us largely through very calm seas. Ironically it was this calm that brought about the biggest storm we faced. From the U.S. vantage point, it seemed our mission ship was not making progress—that the divine wind was not blowing our ship forward.

In February of 1990, Christian Reformed World Missions (CRWM) took up a proposal to phase down the Japan mission by attrition to one missionary so that CRWM could concentrate on less costly, more fruitful fields. The proposal was not precipitous. No missionary would be asked to leave. Any missionary who left would simply not be replaced. To us, it seemed like our mission ship had been caught in a terrible storm and was in danger of sinking. We felt abandoned by our sending church. Didn't they understand the tremendous need for missions in Japan—that the small Japanese church needed our help long term to reach the lost millions of that country? We felt desperate.

We strongly appealed to CRWM not to approve the proposal. While making a case for our financial responsibility, we also argued that missions should not be evaluated by a bang-for-the-buck mentality. Admitting that the Japan mission could not measure up to the rapid growth statistics of some other fields, we questioned whether the work of the Holy Spirit can be measured quantitatively. After all, where would the Tiv church in Nigeria be today if the missionaries to Tivland had been recalled in 1930 because that church saw such little growth for the first few decades?

We weathered the storm, but, in the end, it was not the mission's response but the Reformed Church in Japan's appeal that prolonged the life of the Japan mission. The RCJ leaders succeeded in getting CRWM to see the Japan mission situation through Japanese eyes—to understand that within the Japanese context the Christian Reformed Church in North America-Reformed Church in Japan (CRJM-RCJ) cooperative church planting effort had been unusually fruitful. When they heard the news of the proposal to phase down the mission, they acted swiftly and decisively. They sent the moderator of their general assembly to the Christian Reformed Church synod to appeal, which he did—with eloquence, passion, and wisdom. He shattered the stereotype many Americans had of Japanese as people who hide their feelings and don't speak their minds. He invited the CRWM leaders to visit Japan to dialog with the leaders of the RCJ there. The dialog took place in Tokyo. The CRWM leaders agreed that God had indeed been blessing the joint CRJM-RCJ church-planting efforts and recommended that the Japan mission not be phased down.

I was very grateful both to God and to my Japanese colleagues that our mission was allowed to continue. As we went through the throes of the debate, however, I had to acknowledge that God's will could be accomplished in Japan even if the CRJM missionaries all returned. When I prayed, "Your will be done," I had to be prepared for the possibility that God's will would be accomplished through a plan to which I was opposed. That did not happen. The plan to downsize was set aside, but, ironically, in the fourteen years that have elapsed since then, the Japan mission along with the rest of CRWM has downsized, just not as rapidly as the 1990 plan envisioned. Who knows? Maybe the gospel breakthrough in Japan for which we have prayed so long will come only after the foreign missionaries are gone. It happened that way in China; it could happen that way in Japan too. Or perhaps all this mission retrenchment is a sign of diminished mission vision, and what we should really be doing is getting on our knees and praying for the divine wind to blow.

Sailing Home—Last Leg of the Voyage

So why did we leave Japan? It was not an easy decision, but eventually we sensed that God was gently asking us to sail in another direction. Our children, now all in the United States, and our parents were wondering when we would return to the States. It became increasingly clear that these wonderings arose out of certain needs and that Sandy and I were best equipped to meet those needs. The needs were still many in Japan, and the number of Christian workers was not nearly large enough, but who else could fill the role of son and daughter to our parents or the role of father and mother to our children? We prayed, "God, if you want us to return to the States, please open one door for us," and a door opened in an unexpected place. In May 2000, the Calvin Theological Seminary Board of Trustees decided to create a new faculty administrative position: dean of students and international student advisor. Within days, I was being encouraged by several people to apply for this new position, and, less than three months later, I began my new assignment at Calvin Seminary—convinced that God had led us here. It was difficult to leave the work in Japan, but it is God's work, not ours, and he continues to move the Japanese church forward without us.

Conclusion

The realization that my ministry is all God's ministry has shaped my attitude toward ministry in many ways. It has inhibited my innate desire to take credit for any "success" in ministry. It has filled me with gratitude—that God chooses me to be his partner in ministry, that he blessed others and built churches through my efforts. It has taught me that the first prerequisite for ministry is faithful obedience to God. Knowing that all spiritual life and growth are the work of the Holy Spirit has curbed my impatience regarding slow church growth in Japan. Even though the results were not explosive, I never lost hope or confidence that Christ would build his church in that country. Christ's promise that he would build his church pushed me on. John's vision of "a great multitude that no one could count, from every nation, tribe, people and language standing before the throne and in front of the Lamb" (Rev. 7:9) pulled me forward. God has been in all our work in Japan—energizing us, empowering us, leading us. Sailing with God has been and still is a wonderful kamikaze adventure.

For Further Reflection

Compare the story of Pentecost in Acts 2 with quieter "mini-Pentecosts" such as we find in John 20:19-23 and Acts 19:1-7. Do these and other passages support Sytsma's testimony that God's Spirit carries us "sometimes like a gentle breeze, sometimes with amazing force?" Those interested in further reflection on such questions may want to consult *A Theology of the Holy Spirit* by Frederick Dale Bruner.

What are specific ways in which you and your congregation are "learning the ropes" in terms of maintaining your relationship to God, continuing your education, working as a team, and facing conflict in healthy ways?

CHAPTER 9

The Pastor as Pilgrim

Cecil Van Niejenhuis

In this narrative, Cecil Van Niejenhuis refers to "the slow-moving God of the Scriptures." But, in keeping with the wisdom of the Bible, he understands that "the Lord is not slow in keeping his promise, as some understand slowness" (2 Peter 3:9). Instead, the "slowness" of God is for the sake of holy purposes that can be accomplished only over time and as part of a story—the epic story of the Scriptures.

Some preachers think quickly and clearly while on their feet. Every once in a while I'm a preacher like that, but more often than not, my thinking clears up when I'm sitting down, either at my desk, or behind the steering wheel of my car. That's when I sort through what I should have said, or plan what I will say the next time I run into whatever it was I ran into.

It's a gradual process, ruminating over remarks made, or marinating some well-seasoned and witty words that will strike so and so's ears with the finality of a chairperson's gavel. End of discussion. Settled and binding. That's the theory, anyway.

That's not the reality.

It should be so simple. It isn't.

It should be so efficient. It isn't.

I should have answers. I should have solutions. Sometimes I do. Many times I do not—and certainly not instantly.

As I look back on things I have learned over the years, I especially remember one comment and one question, separated by nearly a decade, both of which flustered me at the time. Together, they have led me to reflect on the nature of my role as a pastor and the nature of this thing we call the church. It's been a gradual process, this reflection. It's been a long story. That is precisely the way it needs to be.

From Survival to Greener Pastures

In the early years of my pastoral life, my first instinct was simply survival. I recall when I'd been in my first charge for four years. Four years! That seemed an accomplishment. I can remember thinking that my first summer assignment to a congregation had been a major test. Young and even younger-looking, I had turned twenty-three years old that summer and marvelled at the miracle of survival. Would the congregation survive? Would I? We did. I was convinced that only God knew how.

Then it was a year-long internship. A full year in the same church! Would my insecurities be unmasked and my inadequacies underlined? This was a church over which Jesus Christ was the head! This was a church for which the Holy Spirit surely had plans! My plans were more modest than the Spirit's. Survival.

A year went by. The senior pastor affirmed my gifts. The congregation was encouraging. To my surprise, I had not only survived but had grown and was now ready, as far as the church was concerned, and, I trusted, as far as God was concerned, to be ordained into full-time ministry.

It was a preacher's market that summer. Eight churches extended calls in my direction. Others were waiting in the wings. What to do? A pastor who was near retirement offered some advice: "Your call is to the ministry. God wants you to work in his vineyard. But as to which vine you choose to tend, well, that's entirely up to you. You can fulfill God's will no matter where you go."

I experienced those words as liberating. To honor our sense of duty, we narrowed our choices to the three congregations that had been vacant for at least one full year. Perhaps I could think about more than survival. Perhaps I could think about which church we preferred!

With a mentality perhaps closer to Lot's than to Abraham's, we chose the one that looked well-watered and lovely, like the garden of the Lord. Then we discovered we had walked into a dense, almost impenetrable jungle. This was a congregation in which there was an altogether uncivil war raging, but there had been no angel waving a sword and preventing us from going there. The survival mode once again became preeminent.

Those first years were formative. They were filled with the weekly crisis of sermon deadlines, the fascinating stories of God's family members, and the daunting necessity of standing firm and even confronting those who were undermining the fellowship. I learned the leisurely pace at which relationships develop and trust is built. Teaching, discipling, and avoiding getting caught in the crossfire—somehow, through it all, God was at work. The church grew not only in numbers but also in grace as those at odds with each other learned to live in a genuine, if somewhat precarious, truce. That's another story however.

There were times when I wondered how I had chosen to go to that place. There were times when I wondered why God had sent me there. Perhaps there might be some greener pastures.

The phone began to ring. It seemed like every church was located in Macedonia! Remembering that minister's words about God's vineyard, I chose to accept a new challenge—and did so with a great sense of freedom as well as openness to God's leading. This new congregation was in a rural community about as far from my first congregation in miles as it was in terms of sheer beauty. The one was a historic village with charm and old society graces; majestic trees and scenic gardens. The other was what we politely called "rustic." The church building was old and in need of repair. It was ten miles from the nearest town. The parsonage was sandwiched between that church building on the one side, and the cemetery on the other. The road was gravelled. The prairie winds created storms of dust.

But the people!
And the sky!
And the spaciousness!

As any prairie-born person will tell you, the beauty of the prairie is subtle. It grows on you. The wideness and the wildness have a way of invading your senses and converting your urban sensibilities. It happens gradually (doesn't everything?) until one day you suddenly realize that your eyes have been opened to a wonder that you had not always considered wonderful.

The Comment and the Question

As we stood and greeted people at the back of church that Sunday when we announced our move to the west, we heard many voices tinged with sadness, some with wistful encouragement for our adventure, and one voice that was as lethal as the handshake was limp: "You sure chose a hole in the ground."

In my mind, I heard myself say, *Excuse me? Did I hear you say what I think I heard you say?* But in reality, I said nothing. I was flustered, rather taken aback, and simply stunned.

I tried to be positive. Was this person indirectly expressing her anger at my leaving? Was this a backhanded compliment, perhaps? Reason led me to face the truth. There was nothing redemptive about the remark. It was simply nasty and intended to make me conscious of the fact that I had made a rather foolish choice. Stupid is as stupid does.

Later, something else occurred to me. Whatever that comment may have intended to say to me, it certainly said something disdainful about the congregation to which I was headed. A hole in the ground? The comment was not only disdainful of the location, but also of the kind of people who live in such locations. I wondered what the people in Jerusalem thought when the apostle Paul headed off to Lystra and Derbe and Iconium. Turkish delight, anyone?

Years later, the sting of that comment returned. It was shortly after we'd moved to a new city and to another congregation. This was an established congregation, nearly ninety years old—a church whose membership included a significant segment of seniors and a church whose members all commuted to its virtually inner-city location.

The area pastors and their spouses were gathered for an evening of relaxed fellowship. It was an opportunity to meet new colleagues and renew old friendships. As it turned out, it was also an occasion for me to deal with a rather pointed jab. The voice asked the question so directly it stilled the room. "What's a preacher like you doing in a church like that?"

A preacher like me.

And a church like that.

Such comments and questions are tips of an iceberg. There's much more hidden than the surface would indicate. In fact, they relate to a whole number of dynamics with which preachers and congregations wrestle quite regularly. They relate to the question of identity. Who am I as a pastor? What's my role within a congregation? What should be my personal and professional goals? What about goals for a congregation? Identity is something shaped by external forces, and it is something internal, which has formative, shaping power that influenced our patterns of pastoral behavior and the choices we make—such as where we end up serving a congregation.

The presumption of both the comment and the question is that the privilege of choice should lead to the experience of choiceness. Choiceness is seen as a growing church, a church with thriving programs and a progressive membership, a church that is effective in its ministries and efficient in its administration, and a church building that is inviting and located within reach of civilization.

Of course, there is also a presumption about the kind of personal and professional goals that a preacher would naturally have. If one's first charge might be to a rather isolated congregation, or a less desirable type of congregation, a second or third charge ought to feel something like a promotion. Perhaps it should be a larger congregation or a larger urban center or a church with an adequate number of staff. This ought certainly to be true if you are a preacher with recognized ability!

The advice offered me by that retiring colleague now seems not so much liberating as simplistic. Deciding where to live and work is much messier than he suggested. To say that one's call is to the vineyard of God and that the choice of vine is strictly a choice of preference does not honor the struggle within one's own heart and conscience. Sorting through my own motivations, they seem always to be a tangled web of good intentions and selfish ego, of servanthood and control, of willingness to surrender and resentment at the need to sacrifice. I, together with the members of the congregation in which I serve, am a very human being. The road toward maturity, the kind of spiritual maturity that Paul teaches, is a road with twists and turns, long and winding. It's a gradual process, and it's a gradual process for all of us.

While search committees are highly thorough and cleverly creative in presenting the appeal of their particular community with respect to all the opportunities for a rich and varied life experience, one wonders just where the appeal to our desire for the "good life" intersects with our desire to honor the call of God. Is there a certain definition of the good life that has come to be accepted as worthy of our pursuit and that has displaced a sense of pursuing the call of God that includes sacrifices of what conventionally are considered "prime locations?" Saying goodbye to a well-regarded, program; to a rich, and numerically growing church; and moving to a less desirable community might be considered a particularly poignant wave offering.

Dynamics of the choosing process aside, in every actual choice in life, the consequences never reveal themselves fully until after the commitment has been made. Pastors learn firsthand, whether married or single, about the nature of making promises. From this day on, at least for a few years, we walk through life together with our congregations, for better and for worse.

No matter where we happen to be, we pastors are involved in the life stories of people. We are permitted to share in very tender moments such as birth and marriage and confession and reconciliation. We are permitted to share in fragile moments such as illness, grief, and relationships gone awry. We are even permitted to speak the truth when it hurts to speak the truth. We have front-row seats as we watch people of all ages struggle to mature. If we stay somewhere long enough, we may even be privileged to see the return of those who have fallen away. These are gradual things: The stories of people's lives unfold over time and across the years.

No matter where we happen to be, the members of the church of Jesus are people. They are extraordinarily ordinary people who pleasantly surprise and who regrettably disappoint. They are the people whom God loves, and they are the people through whom God chooses to minister to the world and whom God calls to be his representatives in the world. This simple fact convinces me that God is not nearly as interested in efficiency as we often are. In fact, God takes a peculiar pleasure in doing things rather unconventionally when compared with human standards and presumptions.

This appeals to a certain subversive part of my character, and it is a rather consistent feature of the kingdom's coming! God chooses what is weak and foolish; he chooses people in out-of-the-way places and with imperfect pedigrees to accomplish some wonderful things. What's more, it's often hard to measure just how we're doing. The way of the Spirit is a mysterious one, both in terms of the way the Spirit stirs and shapes me, and in the way the Spirit stirs and shapes the church of Jesus.

Pilgrims in Vanity Fair

We've been inundated over the last years with tools and more tools for measuring the effectiveness of church programs and ministries, for measuring the effectiveness and vitality of worship, for measuring virtually every facet of this thing called the church. Well-intentioned and useful as such tools often are, I am convinced that with their use something unintended has gradually happened. That unintended something is that the standards of the world of business have become the accepted standards for the church and for pastors in the church. An entrepreneurial, market mentality has come to dominate our understanding of the church.

Successful churches are churches that grow numerically.

Successful churches are churches that connect supply with demand.

Successful churches create ministries that address the needs of the consumer.

Standards for measurement are typically statistical in nature.

Are numbers important? They can be, but that's all. I believe that when our primary model for the church is a market model, for all the benefits we gain in terms of efficiencies and numerical growth, we end up losing something that is even more essential: the notion that we are a pilgrim people and that the stories of our lives find their place within the grand story that the Scriptures tell. We're also losing a sense of our identity as pastors; gravitating toward a corporate management model. I'm sure God appreciates gifted administrators because those gifts are his to give! There's no doubt that God is about the business of redeeming his creation. He has a vast and glorious enterprise that he directs and in which he employs his people. God's venture, however, is revealed within the context not of a chart but of a story.

That comforts me. The very nature of a story encourages me to exercise patience with myself and with the church. It also encourages patient trust in the slow-moving God of the Scriptures! The kind of measuring that seems most appropriate for our community is the kind of deep, soul-inspiring measuring that is actually impossible to complete: It's measuring the immeasurable dimensions of God's love in Christ Jesus, as Paul puts it in his letter to the Ephesians. It's the kind of impossible measuring that God encouraged Abraham to try when he suggested that Abraham count the stars of the sky.

Stories by their very nature, unfold slowly—especially stories of epic proportions and length, especially stories such as the story of the Scriptures, that are concerned with character development and with a plot that covers the ages. Because my identity as a person and as a pastor is rooted within this story, and because I understand the identity of the church as being rooted in this epic story, comments and questions that presume standards of performance rooted in a contemporary market model jar me. They simply cannot tell the whole story.

I am leery of any book, any person, or any program that promises:
Grand results in an instant.
Forty days to a more focussed, blessed life.
Four steps to spiritual maturity.
Ten life lessons that will change you forever.

I try not to let such claims be intimidating, either to myself or to the congregation. Pastoring is about walking with people. Walking. Pastoring is not so much preaching to people as it is preaching among them. It's about telling a story to people who love to hear a story. Good stories have a way of unfolding themselves to listeners in layers of meaning. It's a process. It's gradual, and it does lead to the kind of maturing that Paul speaks about. Ultimately, it does lead to the kinds of grand numbers that God speaks about!

It's been ten years already, and a preacher like me is still in "that" church.
What am I doing in a church like that?

By God's grace, I'm telling the story—the same old story that seems each time I tell it, more wonderfully sweet. I'm reaping the fruits of long-term acquaintances and friendships built on trust. I'm finding myself able to speak meaningfully, redemptively, and pointedly at funeral services. I'm living through times of members' long absences and God's apparent silences, and then seeing these people return. I'm watching the baton of faith passed from one generation to the next and witnessing a new generation of leaders emerge and mature. I'm exploring new dimensions of spiritual vibrancy and new dimensions of ministry. I'm developing a deepening commitment to the mission of God. I'm building community by cultivating the fruit of the Holy Spirit's presence. As a pastor, I'm discovering that the longer I stay, the more fully I need to wrestle with my own weaknesses and to become a partner in the process of spiritual maturation.

This is a good life. It was here all along. This life can be found wherever we walk—aware that we walk before the face of God. Walking before the face of God is, it seems to me, a rather choice location.

For Further Reflection

Van Niejenhuis reports that after a few years in his first charge, he began to think, *Perhaps there might by greener pastures.* What presumptions and presuppositions are at work in your view of your congregation and location and how biblical are they? For example, does the "slowness" of God shape your expectations? One valuable resource for such reflections is Eugene H. Peterson's book, *Under the Unpredictable Plant: An Exploration in Vocational Holiness.*

CHAPTER 10

On Being a Servant Leader: A Conversation

Richard E. Williams

Reverend Richard E. Williams has been serving at Pullman CRC, a racially/ethnically integrated church (30 per cent Dutch-American and 70 per cent African-American) on the South Side of Chicago, for 22 years. Rick sat down with Mr. Grant Elgersma, a new member of Pullman Church and writer for www.cultureisnotoptional.com, to discuss some of the things he has learned about servant leadership from his many years in the ministry. Editor Joel Kok took the liberty of adding a few questions of his own.

Grant Elgersma: It's rare for a pastor to stay with one congregation for more than ten years. Were you expecting to stay that long when you first started at Pullman Church?

Rick Williams: No, not at all. I thought that maybe after five years, I'd be moving on. Being at Pullman Church for twenty-two years wasn't something that I'd mapped out. But as I look back, I can see the Lord was leading the way. I really needed to settle down and establish some roots somewhere as I learned to serve the community God has called me to, and that takes time. So, in terms of identifying and developing my skills as a pastor, and also in terms of developing community, it's been good for me to stay here so long.

If I had thought when I first came in that I'd be here twenty-two years, I would have thought that it would become boring or that I'd get tired. What has happened is that I've grown. I've gone through different changes, and I've seen changes in the lives of the people I've known here. There's a built-in freshness to my life here. I've been privileged and honored to be part of major events in the lives of many people: birth, baptism, profession of faith, graduation, weddings, sickness, death, and so forth. New people come with new ideas, and I encourage them to express those ideas. That way, I experience the newness of the Lord all the time.

G.E.: When you started at Pullman Church, did you have a sense of what you could bring? Did you have a feeling for how long it would take to develop or accomplish what you were hoping to develop here?

R.W.: I heard somebody say that it takes about ten years to get the lay of the land and win the trust of people. I certainly think that the first year you're in an established church is not a time to try to make a lot of changes.

As a servant leader, you need to spend at least that first year listening and learning, being very careful about instigating changes without the people's consent. So, if you ask me, I didn't have a plan. I just took it one day at a time. The months rolled on into years and, so, here I am.

Joel Kok: Rick, let me follow up on your statement, "I didn't have a plan." Many voices say planning is essential for ministry. Others say planning can get in the way of actually doing ministry in terms of the "givens" of pastoral work, such as studying, praying, preaching, visiting, and so forth. What do you think about planning?

R.W.: Don't get me wrong. I didn't have a plan in terms of a personal goal for staying at Pullman a certain number of years, but the church has always had ministry plans. Also, I've gone to seminars and conferences, and we found the Missions Analysis Projection program of Home Missions to be helpful. You're on to something with your question, though, because the structures or "givens" built into pastoral life have served me well. I don't try to reinvent the wheel.

Also, I've found that when you go to conferences, you need to process the lessons through your own people. The answers for Pullman Church are not at some conference. They are at Pullman.

J.K.: Can you give an example of that?

R.W.: Yes. It has to do with a suggestion my wife, Amalia, made about combining our Sunday school with a boys-and-girls-club program that met on a weekday every other week. Running both programs, we struggled to find leaders, and we struggled to get kids to come. I didn't want to make too many changes on my own, so I gathered all the program leaders to discuss my wife's idea. At first, there was some resistance, but we kept talking and thinking and praying together, and as we continued to meet, enthusiasm began to build. Soon, these leaders were on a roll, and I didn't even need to attend all the meetings. We wound up combining a meal and choir with the other programs and holding them all on Wednesday nights. I could give more details, but, the point is, the ideas came from the people involved. We could have called a consultant, but the answer was in the congregation when we took the time to listen to each other.

It's been a wonderful thing to see. My job was to bring them together and help them ask the right questions. The feedback and fine tuning continue, and God teaches us on the way. From my side, this was all unintended. I've learned to become a process-oriented leader. I bring information, but the people make decisions, including times when they vote me down! We do have a vision statement and all that good stuff, but the main thing is that we've done it together.

J.K.: What can you tell us about the specific challenges of leading a multiracial church?
R.W.: We've had tensions especially in the areas of worship and music, which is true of most churches, I guess. But race adds another layer to the tension, and sometimes we can't get beyond it. I've learned how to compromise and adjust, and I've learned that I can't solve all problems. Some things have blown up in my face, and I've learned not to make the same mistake again.

I preach about racism and the mystery of the gospel's bringing Jews, Gentiles, and all peoples together. I usually don't mount a frontal attack when race issues arise. I try to bring people together to share human struggles and testimonies. For example, for almost a year now, I've been part of a mixed-race group made up of people from various Christian Reformed churches who talk about their favorite biblical characters. The different races connected through this discussion. Another time, we were telling stories, and someone brought up a family member with cancer. People from different backgrounds could sympathize from their own experience, and we could begin to create our own story as God's people. Within that story, we can face some of our fears and establish trust. We can win each other over by love, and we can hope for progress because we can see things God has done among us.

G.E.: Even with stories like you've just told, you must have considered moving on at one time or another.
R.W.: Well, I've gotten many inquiries over the years but nothing that I've felt called to. The one serious inquiry to which I almost said yes was also the only one I invited the congregation to be a part of. That was a few years ago. There was a seminary position open at Calvin Theological Seminary (director of field education) that would have allowed me to use my gifts and experience to help train new pastors. Some friends of mine encouraged me to consider it, so I went through the whole interview process and was offered the position. I almost took it, but I decided to let the congregation respond before I made my final decision. I sat around the table on a Sunday evening with over thirty people from the congregation who gave me all kinds of reasons why I shouldn't go! Well, this caught me by complete surprise, but

it was very affirming. The congregation's response became the most important factor in my decision to stay at Pullman Church.

G.E.: It does seem that you are an integral part of the Pullman church community. People feel like you belong intimately to them and to their church.
R.W.: You don't know what people are really feeling until you are led to seriously consider a call elsewhere. That's why I think it's important for pastors to take a call seriously every once in a while because you're testing the Lord and his work where you are and in your heart. I think it's important for the church to struggle with that because some day I will go. I might take another call or retire or die. It's good for people to think every once in awhile about what kind of servant leader meets the particular needs of their church.

G.E.: What are some of the things that helped you achieve the kind of relationship you have with the congregation?
R.W.: Approachability. I have a sense of humor, which communicates approachability. I also try to show an attitude of caring toward people. A pastor-therapist friend of mind told me that he has found out in his ministry that "people want to first know how much you care before they care about how much you know." I have certainly found that to be true in my ministry here.

Integrity. This is not perfection, but trying to walk the talk of loving others. People need to know that I'm not just blowing smoke. I show people that I struggle too. I don't necessarily broadcast it at every opportunity, but if someone is struggling with something, it's good for them to know they're not the only ones. Sharing your struggles communicates the truth that we all need God. A pastor has to be especially careful about what he says and does, though. A pastor can make certain mistakes only once because integrity is very important for enduring in the ministry. Integrity includes keeping your word, keeping appointments, returning calls in a timely manner, and being consistent. When you say you're going to be somewhere at a certain time, you'd better be there. I try to write things down when people set up appointments with me. Usually, I'll take out my planner and pencil in the appointment while I'm standing in front of them. That shows them they're important to me, that their time and concerns are important to me. You have to communicate to people that they matter, that they're important. This is a very tangible expression of God's love. Finally, there's confidentiality—a person with integrity keeps confidences.

Biblical preaching. When you preach, you have to preach to how people listen. Spend lots of time preparing the message, reading, studying, and finding the right illustrations. Also work at storytelling. Keep your ears and eyes open to all forms of media so the crafted sermon speaks to where the people are. I work hard to make sure that the sermon is really good news. I work hard to give messages that major in faith, hope. and love. After all, the thrust of the Scriptures is on freedom and the good news.

Administrative skills. Even though I'm not the most organized person in the world, I have learned a few things about how to keep things running as smoothly as possible. Part of my job is to give information that helps people make good decisions for the church. You need to give people what they need in a timely fashion.

Willingness to say, "I don't know." You don't have to explain everything. You don't have to try to make God logical or plausible so that everything makes perfect sense because sometimes it doesn't make complete sense from our perspective. I try to keep in mind what the apostle Paul says in 1 Corinthians 13:9-10: "For we know in part and we prophesy in part, but when perfection comes, the imperfect disappears."

Peacemaking skills. I am the fourth of nine children, and very early on in my family and at school I was identified as a peacemaker. Over the years, I have not only owned but also developed that particular gift, and it serves me well in the church because I've been caught in the middle of many battles. To be a good pastor, you have to be a diplomat and ambassador, so that, even if some people don't like the decision that was made, they know it was fair.

Flexibility. This is very important. You come out of seminary ready to share your studies, and then you get to church and there's a leak in the ceiling, or you have to supervise the janitor, or you have to stay late to help clean up after a congregational dinner.

Keeping in mind those who are out of sight. It's easy to get so busy with the important affairs that are right in front of you from day to day that you forget about those who haven't been in church for awhile: the sick, the shut-ins, those in prisons, and inactive members. Visitation is very important. The sick and the elderly who are faced with the reality that life could end at any time know the importance of the visit more than I do. Sometimes I get more out of it than they do. I also like to invite others along for the visit, members of the person's family or of the church, so that the sick or elderly person can experience the community of the saints.

Openness to criticism. Even though it's not pleasant to hear criticism, it's important to be open to it. I ask for helpful criticism at council and elders' meetings. It's actually part of the agenda. I've had to learn to listen to everything without going on the attack, becoming defensive, or being rude. You'd love to hear only good things. You'd love to hear you're a wonderful person and perfect in every way, but that's just not the case. So, it's good to ask for helpful criticism. I have also learned to seek the input of certain members of the congregation who see me not only as their pastor but as their friend as well.

Personal devotional time. I set aside large chunks of time for solitude. I need that kind of time to meditate and think and pray. It's important to read through Scripture constantly, not just for the next sermon, so the Word becomes a part of you. Read things that feed your soul.

G.E.: In a lecture you gave at Calvin Seminary in April of 2002, you mentioned that the expectations you have for yourself as a pastor are very much in line with the expectations your congregation has of you. How do you foster an environment that leads to the kind of openness that is necessary for meeting the expectations of Pullman Church?

R.W.: I certainly foster it with the church council. It is my responsibility to come with a clear agenda, with good information that people would not otherwise have if I were not there, and to provide an open process in which people can talk and discuss and make their decision, even if I don't agree with it. Sometimes I've had to say, "I don't agree with this, but we'll have to work and live with this." More often than not, they make better decisions than I would have made myself. So I lean on them. I think it's very important for people to know that, as a pastor, you're not a dictator. You're there because the Spirit of God is working through you and through his people too. Together we come to do the work of the church. That's how I conduct council meetings

The same thing goes for dealing with people outside the council—regular pastoral activities such as getting to know people, working with them in the kitchen, Sunday school, and so forth. People call me for all kinds of things: trouble in a marriage, difficulty with children, anxiety about death—whatever. I try to be there for people.One thing I think I've developed is a sense of knowing when and how to listen without trying to correct or fix. I can hear some heretical stuff from people, and some downright mean stuff, but I've learned to realize when people don't need me to correct them. Sometimes they just want to be heard and to feel like they're appreciated and loved. As a pastor, you have to remember that your job is not just to correct people's theology but to provide them with a safe place where they can express some of their deepest doubts and fears.

G.E.: You seem to be open to learning from people and from your experiences with people over the years. What else have you learned from others, in general, and more specifically from Pullman Church?

R.W.: One thing I've learned is how people process change. I've learned that a lot of our identity is, for better or worse, tied up in how we do things. So, when you think you're just making a simple change, you're tampering with people's senses of who they are. Never underestimate the impact of any change on a system. Even moving a table from one corner to another can raise a lot of fuss in a church or with people.

I've learned to get people's opinions on things the best I can; to get a group sense of things. Get as much approval and consensus as you can because when you're moving ahead as a leader, you want to know that you have most of the people with you. Of course, there are certain things we can't vote on, but there is much room for creativity when it comes to matters of process and implementation.

To be more specific, I have learned to be more reserved when I'm leading worship, which is not easy for me. I'm an entertainer at heart but, for some people, I cross that line between entertainer and worship leader. The elders' regular feedback has helped me to use my ability to entertain in a creative way in the context of worship.

G.E.: Does the kind of informal style of conducting worship have more to do with your own personality, with who you are, or does it come out of principles you believe are important for doing church worship in general?

R.W.: It mostly has to do with who I am. I'm also aware of certain principles. I've gone to worship services that seem so systematic and methodical; I could close my eyes and do it. Yet, when I preach in those churches, and I make a joke, people will laugh in a natural way. When you hear people laugh in a Christian Reformed tradition, you know you've done something good because they're trying their best—even when they know something is funny—not to laugh! I try to respect other people's styles of worship. Especially when I go to other churches, I try to work within the structure there because, for a lot of those churches, it's enough of a change to have me there. So, I don't expect the congregation to learn how to shout, "Amen!" while I'm worshiping with them. I respect how other people do things.

G.E.: How have your expectations for being a pastor changed since you've been at Pullman?

R.W.: It took me a long time, even while being at Pullman Church, to finally say, "Yeah, I've been called to become a pastor. That's who I am. That's what I like to do. That's how God wants me to serve. I haven't missed my calling."

For one thing, I discovered that being a pastor uses all my gifts. For instance, I've taught school—elementary, junior high, adults. I like to teach. I like to visit people. I am philosophically and theologically oriented, and, of course, that's part of my job. I like to take complex things and break them down for ordinary people—but I don't want to be a college professor. I also have some counseling skills—but I don't want to be a full-time counselor. I don't mind doing some janitorial work, either. I wouldn't want to be a full-time janitor—but I don't mind carrying chairs and mopping floors every once in awhile. When I was in seminary, I thought that maybe I'd do a Ph.D., but one of my professors assured me that people do a lot of creative things without having a Ph.D.

I realize now that when I was asking that question twenty-five years ago, it was more out of the sense that maybe a Ph.D. would make me feel better about myself or make people feel better about me—that I would somehow be a great person if I had one. I finally put that idea to rest. What I discovered over the years was that the Lord used my being in the ministry to draw those gifts out of me. He kept me here long enough for me to see my gifts as his servant. He's made good progress with me so that I could finally come to the point where I can say, "Yeah, this is where I belong. I want to be a parish minister. That's where God wants me to be."

It gives me a sense of joy to do what I do, to work until the end of the day—and sometimes in the middle of the night—on what I'm passionate about. We all want to be great. We want to feel like we are good at what we do, and we want to be admired by others. Isn't it great to know who you are and that what you're doing matters? It's very satisfying. We hear of so many people who are dissatisfied with their jobs, but I love my job! I am doing what I've been called to do. I'm glad to be serving in the kingdom that Jesus describes in Mark 10. In God's kingdom, whoever wants to be great must be a servant serving after the example of Christ. Dr. Martin Luther King Jr., in one of his sermons ("The Drum Major Instinct"), said, "everybody can be great because everybody can serve." As a leader of God's people, I am glad to take on the great responsibility of service and to help others serve in their own ways so that they, too, can share in the blessings of God's kingdom. "Praise God, from whom all blessings flow!"

For Further Reflection

In one of their documents, the Christian Reformed church's Sustaining Pastoral Excellence implementation team observes, "Too often pastors have been insufficiently prepared to be effective leaders. Neither the 'passive pastor' nor the 'imposing visionary' model is adequate, but most pastors function (at least implicitly) with one of those two modes and do not have the resources to think of alternative models."

How does Rick Williams provide a resource for an alternative model of leadership? Besides the Mark 10 passage that Williams cites, what biblical passages and themes can guide pastors as leaders? Can pastors avoid "careerism" while also appropriating material from the vast amount of leadership literature available in other fields? Does your congregation have a forum in which the pastor and congregation can discuss practical matters of leadership?